nella sua acuta

attenzione critica...

Con l'affetto di

Luigi *

nov. '00

ANGELS OF YOUTH

* lfontanella@notes.cc.sunysb.edu

Other books by the same author available in English:

From G. to G.: 101 Somnets (New York: Peter Lang, 1996, with Giose Rimanelli), translated from the Italian by Luigi Bonaffini and others.

Hot Dog, a novel (Lewinston, New York, Soleil, 1998), translated from the Italian by Justin Vitiello.

The Transparent Life and Other Poems (Stony Brook, New York: Gradiva Publications, 2000), translated from the Italian by Michael Palma.

Luigi Fontanella

ANGELS OF YOUTH

Edited and Translated from the Italian
by
Carol Lettieri and Irene Marchegiani Jones

Preface
by
Carol Lettieri and Irene Marchegiani Jones

Introduction
by
Rebecca J. West

A Xenos Dual-Language Edition
_____

ᚷ ENOS BOOKS

ISBN 1-879378-43-4 (paper)

Front Cover Illustration: *Portrait of Emma* by Vanni Rinaldi (1988)
Cover Design: Tom Giacalone
Typesetting: Donna Severino, Fort Salonga, New York
This Xenos Books publication was made possible by a gift from
the Sonia Raiziss Giop Charitable Foundation.

Xenos Books
P. O. Box 52152
Riverside, CA 92517-3152
Web site: www. xenosbooks.com
Tel: (909) 370-2094 Fax: (909) 370-2229

Printed in the USA

851.914
F

Acknowledgments

We are very grateful to the author, whose collaboration on this translation has been essential to our entire work. His comments on the translations, his clarification of nuances of the Italian versions of the poems, and his openness to express his literary aims and share personal experiences have proved invaluable in allowing us to bring our translation to completion.

We wish to extend our thanks to the Sonia Raiziss Giop Charitable Foundation of New York for its support of our translation, and to Dr. Karl Kvitko, publisher of Xenos Books, for reviewing our work with attention not only to all of the details and questions usually raised by any translation, but also with a genuine passion for poetry.

Our work could not have been possible without the support and advice of Greg McHolm, who carefully read successive drafts of all of the poems, offering valuable suggestions.

We also thank Caramanica, the publisher of the Italian volume *Ceres*, for permitting the reproduction of the Italian text. *Ceres*, in fact, was published in 1996 in a series entitled *I Transatlantici* dedicated to Italian authors who live and write abroad. We are honored to assist in furthering the goal of promoting Italian literature to a broader audience within the United States.

C. L.   I. M. J.

Table of Contents

Preface

Angels of Youth is a translation of *Ceres*, Fontanella's ninth volume of poetry, originally published in Italian by Caramanica Editore in 1996. The Italian edition garnered two distinguished poetry prizes (the Orazio Caputo in 1998 and the Olindo De Gennaro in 1999) and was the subject of over thirty reviews in prestigious literary journals in Europe and the United States.[1] Devised with an English-speaking readership in mind, the current translation incorporates subtle modifications to the original volume, including a reorganization of the book's structure, omissions of a few poems deemed too obscure for American readers, and the addition of two new uncollected poems, written in 1999. It is our hope that the present translation will increase public interest in a poetry that, while unique, well represents trends and directions in contemporary Italian as well as in Italian-American poetry.[2]

A professor of Italian Literature at the State University of New York, Stony Brook, since 1982, Luigi Fontanella has published several books of poetry, two books of fiction (one, titled *Hot Dog,* has been translated into English), and several works of literary criticism, including *Il surrealismo italiano* (1983), *La parola aleatoria* (1992), and *Storia di Bontempelli* (1997). His poetry has appeared in translation in numerous anthologies published in France, Spain, England, Russia, and the United States.[3] Born in San Severino, a town near Salerno in Southern Italy, Fontanella has lived in the United States since 1976, but has remained a constant "commuter" between the two nations. In 1996, he founded IPSA (the *Italian Poetry Society of America*) with an ambitious plan of promoting Italian poetry in the United States through conferences and translations focusing primarily upon Italian writers living in America. This activity has demonstrated his tireless enthusiasm and energy, qualities that, while often associated with a "typical" Italian personality, in Fontanella's case, are essential to sustaining his rhythm of continual travel between two countries.[4]

One of the underlying themes of Fontanella's poetry is an exploration of the meaning of "roots." Their presence or absence is an issue that obviously concerns those who have chosen to abandon their land of origin, but it is also a universal problem that touches all human beings in times of deconstructed and lost identities. The incessant journeying from one country to another, and therefore from one culture and language to another, remains a constant in Fontanella's poetry, and is evident also in *Angels of Youth,* although here at times within his "constant movement between geographical perspectives" the poet seems to reach a suspension of the journey, a glimpse of permanence and stability.[5]

This newly found permanence is mirrored in the language. In the past, critics have commented on Fontanella's "language manipulation" (Tamburri 1998). The poet's interest in wordplay, including the coining of neologisms and the combining of nouns and adjectives, as well as the use of terms from foreign languages, is more than a mere linguistic adventure for its own sake. It reflects not only Fontanella's multicultural identity and exposure to the literary heritages of different countries, but, more importantly, his authentic search for a personal "idiolect" that defies the misuses of a poetic lexicon as a means of prevarication. Fontanella appears always to be searching for the most primary meaning of words, where sound and significance can be combined in harmony.

In *Angels of Youth,* this linguistic search is less evident, more subtle and refined than before, as if the poet had found, although briefly, a more stable identity of poetic voice and language. As Paolo Valesio noted, "The poems printed in this volume represent a stage of interiorization and calmness. The expressionistic element has remained, but rather than focusing on verbal play, it concentrates on a psychological dimension... Fontanella's peculiar merriment or gaiety is still there, but more tamed; the welcome self-irony remains, but within an atmosphere of recollection and wisdom."[6]

Other critics have commented on the lightness of Fontanella's poetry that is often linked, however, to the complexity of his poetics. Giulio Ferroni writes of Fontanella's "disenchanted transparency" containing a sort of "suspended bitterness toward the elusive signs of our existence" and Rebecca J. West notes that Fontanella is not afraid of singing the "basic themes of lived life" while remaining a "deracinated Italian" who "writes of the betweeness of his existence."[7] The continuous interchange between concrete and psychological worlds, public and private spheres, is also mirrored in the constant blending of the quotidian world with the inner realm of fantasy as evidenced in dreams, memories, and a sort of fantastic philosophy.[8] Valerio Magrelli instead identifies the main motif of Fontanella's poetry as a kind of laceration and *distanziazione* (distancing), linked to the themes of infancy and poetry itself.[9]

In "Nightwatch of the Last Soldier," the poet cites a passage from Novalis:

> *His time was marked by the light,*
> *but night's kingdom has neither time*
> *nor space.*

Rooted in the present while always "resisting time present," the poetry of Luigi Fontanella is marked by a similar paradox. The verse moves from a very particular sense of time and place, where even the date and place of poetic composition are scrupulously recorded for the reader, to a meta-realm of the imagination, where the poet ponders the act of literary creation itself. The poetic diction follows a similar migration from the colloquial and conversational speech of the kingdom of the day to the lyrical, evocative, and abstract language of the night. The book's Muses likewise operate on multiple levels: the personal (the poet's wife, Rosanna; daughter, Emma; and father, Gennaro); the literary (with frequent dedications and allusions to poetic mentors, including Pasolini, Baudelaire, Yourcenar, Saba, Ungaretti, and others); and the mythical (with allusions to Ceres, the goddess of agriculture).

A repeated quest in *Angels of Youth* is to create a poetry that transcends or compensates for "our vile loss/ the breach between our thoughts and written words." This breach is, of course, even more lamentable in the act of literary translation. In transmitting Fontanella's poetry to an English-speaking readership, we have tried as much as possible to mitigate this inevitable "vile loss" by a number of strategies. Our process always began with an attempt to penetrate the opacity of the poem's linguistic surface to reach an understanding of its underlying meaning, which then served as the starting-point for the translation. Our challenge then was to recreate in English – a language whose musicality is not as effortless as in Italian – a poem that mirrored the original, capturing, as much as possible, the complexity of its total effects:

> *I wish that I could touch a poem*
> *that's light and pure,*
> *a little ballad, a refrain, a fairy tale,*
> *a carol or jingle, one of Emma's curls*
> *where sound and sense become*
> *as one a house of glass*

We approached our translation as the transmission of a text, choosing to routinely privilege neither sound nor sense, but to render as best we could our interpretation of the combined poetic, material, and semantic dimensions of the poem.[10] Since the effect of Fontanella's poetry is often achieved through a chance juxtaposition of images (and the serendipitous meanings that are derived from those random pairings), we have tried as much as possible to maintain those ambiguities. Similarly, we have imitated where possible Fontanella's wordplay, use of neologisms, and inclusion of terms in foreign languages.

Our goal has been to remain faithful to the essence of Fontanella's poetry, and, in so doing, we have sought to maintain the humility that is needed in approaching someone else's creative work. We have also realized that despite its unavoidable compromises, translation, like the act of poetic creation itself, is an exploration that can often result in positive, unforeseen encounters. Fontanella's comments on the nature of poetry in "Resisting Time Present" can similarly be applied to translation:

> She does not dance alone but
> with the night-watch of her companions

opening up the chance of a *beyond*
as an extension to the
infinite possibilities of the world
the many comings all together.

Carol Lettieri
Irene Marchegiani Jones

Notes

[1] Some notable reviews include: Domenico Adriano in *Avvenimenti*, January 8, 1997; Mario Fortunato in *L'Espresso*, February 27, 1997; Paolo Valesio, *Yale Italian Poetry*, n.1, Spring 1997; Fabio Doplicher, *Novilunio*, n. 5-6, 1997; Stelio Cro, *Canadian Journal of Italian Studies*, n. 54, 1997; Irene Marchegiani Jones, *Nuova Antologia*, n. 579, October-December 1997; Barbara Carle, *Forum Italicum*, V. XXXI, n. 2, Fall 1997; Giulio Ferroni, *Rivista di Studi Italiani*, XV, n. 2, Dic. 1997; Valerio Magrelli, Ibid.; Alberto Toni, *Galleria*, n. 3, September-December 1997; Giuseppe Panella, *Semicerchio*, n. 18, 1998; Franco Manescalchi, *Erba d'Arno*, n. 71, 1998; Roberto Bertoldo, *Hebenon*, III, n. 2, October 1998; Riccardo Duranti, *L'Immaginazione*, n. 54, 1999.

[2] The two new uncollected poems are *The Branch of the Tree* and *Nightwatch of the Last Soldier*. Some poems from *Ceres* appear in English translation in *The Transparent Life And Other Poems*, trans. Michael Palma. New York: Gradiva Publications, 2000.

[3] Among Fontanella's books of poetry are: *La vita trasparente*, Venice: Rebellato, 1978; *Simulazione di reato,* Manduria: Lacaita, 1979; *Stella Saturnina,*. Rome: Il Ventaglio, 1989; *Round Trip,* Udine: Campanotto, 1991, which won the Ragusa Prize. One of the most recent publications, *Terra del Tempo*, Bologna: Book Editore, 2000, won the prestigious prizes Minturnae and Circe-Sabaudia, whose jury's president was the poet Mario Luzi.

[4] For an analysis of Fontanella's poetry we wish to refer, among others, to Irene Marchegiani Jones' "An Introduction to Italian Poetry in the United States: The *Ars poetica* of Luigi Fontanella," in *Italian History and Culture*, v. 5, 1999. The essay is followed by selected poems from *Ceres* that Marchegiani Jones and Lettieri translated at that time.

[5] Barbara Carle, rev. of *Ceres*, by Luigi Fontanella, *Forum Italicum*, V. XXXI, n. 2, Fall 1997.

[6] Paolo Valesio, rev. of *Ceres*, by Luigi Fontanella, *Yale Italian Poetry*, n. 1, Spring 1997.

[7] Giulio Ferroni, rev. of *Ceres*, by Luigi Fontanella, *Rivista di Studi Italiani*, XV, n. 2, December 1997. Rebecca J. West, cited on the book jacket of *The Transparent Life*, Stony Brook, New York: Gradiva Publications, 2000.

[8] Roberto Bertoldo, rev. of *Ceres*, by Luigi Fontanella, *Hebenon*, III, n. 2, October 1998.

[9] Valerio Magrelli, rev. of *Ceres*, by Luigi Fontanella, *Rivista di Studi Italiani*, XV, n. 2, December 1997.

[10] Barbara Carle makes the distinction between material and semantic aspects of a poem in "On Translating: From Bernam to Pozzi," *Polytext*, V. 14, Winter 1999-2000.

Introduction

Angels of Youth contains most of the poems included in the original Italian volume, *Ceres*, a title that refers not only to a long section and a specific poem in the collection, but more significantly to the goddess of agriculture also known as Demeter. A mythic figure of great resonance, she was honored, along with the god Bacchus, at the Eleusinian mysteries, which celebrated the abduction and return of her beloved daughter Persephone (or Proserpine). This mythic story is about loss: of a daughter, of innocence, of eternal spring. It is also about retrieval and compromise: the acceptance of Necessity, which marks the mortal condition. Fontanella's poetry similarly speaks of loss, but it avoids a purely elegiac tone by rooting itself squarely in the plenitude of the here and now. Time and distance work to separate the poet (and all of us) from beloved places, people, and even memories; his poetry works to conjure up what is, but also what no longer is, or never was, so that it is possible to speak here too of retrieval, of a "consolation of poetry" as powerful as that of philosophy. Myths, such as the story of Ceres and Persephone, have resonated throughout centuries of literature, and Dante, who wrote under the sign of "consolation," beautifully recalled the same tale of loss in his *Commedia* as does Fontanella in his original title, where he wrote in Canto 28 of the *Purgatorio*: "Tu mi fai rimembrar dove e qual era / Proserpina nel tempo che perdette / la madre lei, ed ella primavera" (You remind me of where and how she was, Persephone, when her mother lost her and she lost the Spring). The Eden of perpetual Spring, youth, and unchanging beauty in which Persephone joyfully frolicked with her companions was destroyed by the eruption of desire, as the God of Hades, Pluto, saw, fell in love with, and carried off the virginal flower of girlhood. With the intervention of Jove, Ceres obtained the return of her daughter, but it was a partial retrieval, for Persephone henceforth was to spend only half of her time with her mother, while the other half was to be spent with her husband, Pluto, during which time the earth had to bear the burden of winter's hardships. This emblematic accommodation to partial restitution is in great part the origin of Fontanella's poetry, imbued as it is with his own strong sense of loss.

The perception of loss (either already experienced or anticipated) that characterizes Fontanella's point of view is attributable not only to the shared human condition in which passing time inevitably does its eroding work on youth and on one's past, but also to the poet's particular status as a deracinated Italian and as the father of another young, frolicking daughter who will also leave one day. Fontanella writes about these fundamental themes: the love of origins, of parents, companions, and children; and the betweennesss of his existence, which has stimulated much travel, much leave-taking and returning. The retrieval of lost people and places occurs in small epiphanies, such as when he recognizes his father's face in his own: "Suddenly this morning I recognized you / in my expression / incidentally caught in the mirror" ("Sequence for My Father"). Or, in "For Francesco Paolo Memmo (I)," when the poet remembers a childhood game of rolling a ball down a hill, he perceives "a shift, a double exposure /of something happening now or just having happened / not long ago"; and this little epiphany creates in him a sense of "a rousing call to life." With the poems about or explicitly dedicated to his father, his daughter, his wife, and to other poets, Fontanella establishes a net of relations and a tone of interpersonal communication that draws the reader in, as does the first poem of the collection, entitled "To the Reader." Loss may mark the collection overall, but the dialogical tendency evident in many of the poems – a tendency that is diametrically opposed to hermetic, self-enclosed elegy – opens the poet out onto a shared retrieval that is life-affirming.

There are many beautiful poems in this volume, but perhaps the most beautiful ones are those in the suite "Stanzas for Emma." Here, Fontanella gives his daughter the gift of her own young being, which, due to these poems, she will be better able to revisit in future years. I read these poems from the perspective of a daughter now grown and far from my own young self and innocent beginnings; and I envy Emma this loving, delicate, detailed portrait in words. They not only remind me of what it was like to be very young and entirely open to the future, but they also teach me what fathers (and, by extension, perhaps even my own father) feel and see and live as they experience their tiny offspring. In the first poem of the suite, Fontanella precisely evokes, in almost cinematographic visual detail, the sleepwalking-like night visits to his daughter's cradle: "He moves slowly / lightly shuffling his feet over the floor / he misses the toy chest having tapped / against its wooden rim, lightly touches / the armoire with his fingertips, / here's the edge of the dresser / a passing caress of the ceramic bowl / the imitation antique pitcher the old glass vase / with its dried sorrel flowers, Emma's cradle, and then, and then.... " We can literally feel the exquisite care not to wake Emma in this slow-motion approach to her cradle, as her father gropes his way like a blind man guided by homey, known objects – and by the "radar" of love. The poet's minute observations of his daughter are equally exact and marvelously detailed: her "innocent precision" as her "little hands" swiftly grasp objects that delight her; the "tiny nape of [her] neck" that he looks at as he wheels her in her carriage, and which creates in him a sense of "desperate joy" in "all its unsettling innocence" that "nudges ahead / further ahead... into the thick of the world into the bosom of / every Evil...." The evocations of Emma's wondrous and wonder-filled visage are truly great, as when the poet writes of her "spellbound eyes," her "clear face" as she watches a balloon float away, her "enchanted dreamy air" as she cradles a little bird in her hand, and in a photograph, her "faint smile / that vaguely mixes satisfaction / with a conscious expectation." The poet gives her advice for the future ("You don't know it yet, / nor can you intend it, but be aware / that everything in this world / can be imagined"), and he does his own imagining, of "a land of games and toys / where time happily repeats itself / and all calendars display the same day"; this "great kingdom / where dream and memory color the wind" is where he wishes he could go with Emma. As an inveterate traveler, Fontanella naturally feels deeply the pain of separation occasioned by his many trips away from his daughter, who can "turn [him] to stone / with [her] innocent eyes / and [her] tiny hand / firm and still on [his] suitcase" or whose parting wail follows him throughout his trip "like a wounded dog." Poem XV of the twenty-six-poem suite, called in parentheses "Transpositions," is drenched in a sense of time and its unavoidable march forward. Yet

Emma's innocent trust and laughter bring her father beyond time where he no longer thinks "of the sums and series of days," and instead feels bound up in timelessness: "life as a tender unity / a transposition, a passing breeze / in an All-present / where I live my infinite youth." Through his loving observation of his daughter's unawareness of the ravages of time, and her child's ability to live fully in the present moment, the poet himself throws off the shackles of adult consciousness (if only temporarily) in order to recapture the eternal spring of Ceres' daughter for himself. This epiphanic poem of sweeping vision is a culminating moment in the suite, but it is homey detail that opens and closes "Stanzas for Emma": the "baby elephant / hanging from a heart-shaped balloon" in the introductory poem, and the "Gavroche beret" and "tiny suspenders" that Emma is wearing in the photograph described in the last poem. If, as has been argued in recent criticism, attention to minor detail is most often part of a "feminine" aesthetic economy, then Fontanella has, to my mind, transcended such gendered distinctions, and has as well crossed over the supposed distinctions between paternal and maternal modes of loving, and succeeded in showing the very detailed tenderness of fatherhood, which is, in these poems, no less viscerally felt than the bodily bond between child and mother.

Fontanella moves between countries as an Italian who has lived in the United States for many years but returns very often to his native land. In this collection, he draws on his experience in both countries, and he is also forever moving between past and future, between those people and places of his past that begot him, and those people and places of the present and future by whom and in which he will perhaps be best remembered, particularly his daughter Emma. Although the poems to his daughter speak of time already past, they are future-oriented, as is only right and natural in poems to one's offspring. There are other poems that primarily look back to his "angels of youth"; to the girl who gave him his first kiss, to the time when he wrote in green ink (the color, of course, of youth and hope), to the days when he was "thin and fragile / like a goldfinch lost among the leaves." There is a strongly elegiac quality to these poems, but the voice speaking from the present of remembrance is very connected to the past self, so that the poems are more conjunctive than disjunctive. This continuity between past and present is nowhere more effectively expressed than in "Sequence for My Father," in which the poet's father, Gennaro, who died in 1970 (the poem is dated June/December 1987) reappears, so to speak, in an expression on the mirrored face of his son: "a somber gaze over / your cheerful smile." The yawning gap between the living son and the dead father, who is perhaps "tired of death" and who therefore "reappear[s] in someone else's face," is bridged, and absence becomes presence once more. The "somber gaze" superimposed over the "cheerful smile" is a typically oxymo-ronic, *chiaroscuro* image, of the kind that appears throughout the volume. There is a bittersweet quality to many of the poems, which capture a sensibility divided between past and future, innocent beginnings and the heavy weight of accumulated experience.

The colloquially lyrical, often autobiographically inspired images of many of the poems included in the first two sections, "Ceres" and "Stanzas for Emma," the accessibility of their main themes, and the strongly communicative thrust underlying them do not, however, depend on a poetics of transparency. The connection between experience and language is tenuous at best, an impossible goal at worst. In the strongly meta-poetic third section, "Ars Poetica," Fontanella writes in the liminal poem of "our vile loss / the breach between our thoughts and written words." Writing is an arduous and painful process, a "loss achieved / while becoming thought." It can "reveal to others / something not known to them / unknown even to ourselves / something just discovered or now envisioned." But that "something" can just as well "abandon" us as "invade" us, so that there is no certain epiphanic mechanism that can be made to function during poetic creation. The final section of the volume, "Ballads and Songs," opens with a wish: "I wish I could touch a poem / that's light and pure... where sound and sense become / as one... I wish my verse could become a universe / and everything would find its place again." Time, the limits of expression, displacement, and loss all militate against the fulfillment of this wish, but the poet does not for this reason stop seeking that home in language in which everything (and everyone) might find its place once more. The poems of these final sections reveal the difficult process of excavation beneath the often seemingly effortless constructions of *mots justes* and airy imagery of which the less self-conscious poems are made. Fontanella's poetry is rooted in both a profound critical awareness of the labor of poetry, and a wide embrace of life's labors – and joys, all of which merge in his "pure azure memory." Ceres might well rejoice, for here nothing has been lost for good.

Rebecca J. West
July 2000

ANGELS OF YOUTH

Giovani non si nasce,
giovani si diventa, quando si può.

<small>MASSIMO BONTEMPELLI</small>

Al Lettore

Fra due tangenti oscure
senz'amore di comunicazione
brusìo meccanico, palcoscenico.
Facile cambiare d'equilibrio, umore, postazione
macchie d'un tempo invertebrato. Nessuno,
tranne me, potrà documentarne
lo sbrindellìo disperso
scorie sbadate, sbandate... ripassa
lo stesso bus di poco fa che chiude ogni
speranza di spezzare l'assedio.
Dunque, fraterno ipocrita lettore,
nulla di nuovo. Ti riconfermo
che Tutto avvenne per sbaglio o imitazione.

To the Reader

Between two indistinct poles
with no desire to communicate
a machine-like buzz, a proscenium.
Easy to alter the balance, mood, stance
traces of an invertebrate time. No one
but me can record
the scattered shreds
the careless waste dispersed... the same bus
from a moment ago comes around again
ending all hopes of lifting the siege.
And so, my fraternal, hypocritical reader,
nothing's changed. I can confirm
that Everything has happened by error or imitation.

CERES

Vorrei parlarti, amore,
di come un attimo
si fa spasimo e scintilla
oltre il gesto
e il pensiero d'amarti.

CERES

I wish to tell you, my love,
how an instant turns
to spasm and spark
*   beyond the act*
and thought of loving you.

Inwood

Mute organizzate cineserie
fermo pulsare di foglie dolenti
di fronte a me sgomento che scrivo, dimentico
del chi sono e chi vivo
un attimo nuovo già vela il precedente
e son qui a ricalcare
orme che Tempo sospende.
Freddo, noia, stordimento.
Amo questa quieta neve che scende.

New York, dicembre 1987

Inwood

Mute, orderly chinoiserie
steady pulse of poignant leaves
facing me as I write, amazed at forgetting
who I am and who I am living
a new instant already veils the preceding one
and I am here to retrace
footprints suspended by Time.
Cold, bored, stupefied.
How I love this quiet, falling snow.

New York, December 1987

Erano ragazzi quelli che giocavano
laggiù, oltre l'inferriata. Uno di loro,
certo il più ostinato, batteva
uno stecco contro la ringhiera:
un colpo secco e ripetuto
per ogni combustione soffocata
nel brusìo che tramava intorno.
Ma poi d'improvviso si udì un rapido
scalpiccìo, un farfuglìo di foglie e rami secchi,
un brivido, forse una serpe in fuga
o forse un ragazzo sui pattini
apparso scomparso ai miei occhi.

Inwood Park, New York, aprile 1987

They were just kids, playing
down by the fence. One of them,
the most obstinate for sure, kept beating
a stick against the iron railing:
one dull, rhythmic stroke
for every spark smothered out
by the rustling buzz all around.
Then suddenly a swift shuffling
was heard, a murmur
of leaves and dry branches,
a shudder, a serpent fleeing perhaps
or perhaps a boy on roller skates
appearing disappearing before my eyes.

Inwood Park, New York, April 1987

Affacciato da questa ovale altura
dove tutto frana e sfuma
            dovunque
in digradante armonia
ogni cosa richiede
d'essere nominata in dettaglio
o cancellata in pura visione d'insieme
un trenino elettrico quello che scivola
piano in silenzio laggiù
su rotaie di gomma
e poco più che giocattolini le macchine
che sfilano senza rumore in lontananza.
Qui tuttanatura s'accascia in spettaccolo
imminente, e muta
pulsa, respira.

Monte Porzio, 14 aprile 1987

Looking out from this oval summit
where everything fades and gives way
                    everywhere
in descending harmony
everything clamors
to be named in detail
or erased in a single sweeping vision
the little electric train slowly
gliding down on its rubbery tracks
and cars no more than tiny toys
silently parading by in the distance.
Here all-nature collapses into spectacle –
imminent and mute
it pulses, it breathes.

Monte Porzio, April 14, 1987

Padre-sequenza
(Per Gennaro Fontanella 1911-1970)

Ti penso stasera fra macerie
lordate di sangue innocente
cementosi interstizi d'allucinanti
esattezze gratuite violenze, mentre guardo
alla geografia sgarbata e rapida e sporca
di questa città del futuro già morta.
Mi avresti mai immaginato qui? eppure
che grande impostore il tempo!
Attaccarmi a quel tuo dito nodoso
che mi portava in giro per il mondo.

1.
Mio padre ebbe molti amici nemici
ne ricordo uno in particolare di nome Grossi
soffriva anche lui d'ipertensione
e di altri acciacchi, forse;
scimunito munito d'un sorriso melenso
ti parlava sempre di rimedi e medicine
da lui dottamente esperite
sottilmente compiacendosi, così,
di quest'amministrazione dell'altrui salute
e forse anche pensando meglio a te che a me.
Ma poi anche lui morì.

2.
Stamattina ti ho improvvisamente riconosciuto
in una mia espressione
casualmente catturata allo specchio
in rimbalzo veloce atroce
nella sua nuda comunicazione:

Sequence for My Father
(To Gennaro Fontanella 1911-1970)

Tonight I think of you among these ruins
stained with innocent blood
mortared chasms of dazzling
precision pointless violence – while I regard
the coarse, dirty, and rushed geography
of this city of the future already dead.
Could you ever have imagined me here? And yet
what a great imposter time is!
If only I could hold onto your gnarled finger
that once took me all around the world.

1.
My father had many friendly enemies.
I remember one in particular named Grossi,
he suffered from hypertension too
and other aches and pains, perhaps;
foolhardy and armed with a fatuous smile,
forever talking about the medications
and treatments he had been clever enough to try
gaining thus a subtle gratification
from ministering to the health of others
and perhaps thinking "better you than me."
But later he died too.

2.
Suddenly this morning I recognized you
in my expression
incidentally caught in the mirror
in a quick double-take appalling
in the nakedness of its communication:

lo sguardo triste sul tuo
sorriso sempre ottimista.
Possibile che debba capirti meglio oggi
dopo quasi vent'anni trascorsi un po'
lontano, un po' solo, un poco egoista?

3.
Mi scopro a ripensarti all'età mia di adesso
cogliendo con orrore la spietatezza del tempo
e la pochezza che mi resta. Nel '54
con già quattro figli da sfamare partivi per il lavoro
ogni mattina in lambretta
senza cappotto
proteggendoti con fogli di giornale
che t'infilavi sotto la giacchetta.

4.
Troppo presto ci mancasti
e forse oggi sei stanco d'esser morto
ma vedi, or non è molto, da me promosso
ritornato appari in un altro volto
che ha un po' di te
e un po' di me addosso.

Monte Porzio-New York-Monte Porzio, giugno/dicembre 1987

a somber gaze over
your cheerful smile.
Could it be that I understand you better today
after spending almost twenty years some
distance away, a bit lonely, a bit selfish?

3.
I find myself thinking about you at my age now
recognizing in horror the mercilessness of time
and how little I have left; in '54
already with four children to feed, you'd leave for work
every morning on your Lambretta
no coat
slipping newspaper pages
under your thin jacket like a shield.

4.
You left us too soon
and maybe now you're tired of death
but, you see, it hasn't been that long, at my urging
you reappear in someone else's face
that has in it a little of you
a little of me.

Monte Porzio-New York-Monte Porzio, June/December 1987

Solo il bruciare vale
l'attizzarsi dell'incendio
il crepitìo vario e feroce
il suo inizio spavaldo, l'attimo
che immediatamente precede
lo scoppio, la fiamma, la vampa
improvvisa dei sensi tutti.
Mi dà noia e disgusto
il rimanente, la grigia paccottiglia:
la fredda cenere senza orizzonte
il nauseante disfacimento.
Penso alla legna che c'è in cantina
quanta ce n'è rimasta, quanta bisognerà
consumarne nei prossimi giorni,
a quanta energia in attesa
occorrerà attingere volta per volta
perché fiamma si rifaccia fiamma.

Monte Porzio, gennaio 1988

Only the blazing matters,
the stoking of the fire,
the crackling so fierce and sundry,
its defiant start, that moment
just before
the flash, the flame, the senses
suddenly all ablaze.
To me all the rest
is boredom and disgust, gray rubble:
chilled ashes with no horizon,
a nauseating decay.
I think of the wood down in the basement,
of how much is left, how much we'll need
to burn over the next few days,
how much dormant energy
we'll need to draw upon time after time
to make the flame be flame again.

Monte Porzio, January 1988

Per amore

Abbiamo riposto i nostri vecchi sogni
in cantina, vicini tra loro
si faranno buona compagnia...
Si racconteranno i nostri antichi splendori
le nostre miserie
e le tante perle che regalammo
a chi forse inutilmente amammo.
Immagini ninnoli carte e parole:
a vederli ora rimescolati
patetici sembrano, e odiosi
nell'odore di morte di questa
ripetizione. Passato è il loro tutto e niente
e noi forse altro non sappiamo che ripeterci
vivendoci meglio e meno
contemporaneamente.
Perché tutto, Rosanna, s'addiziona
e nulla si cancella. Proprio come disse il poeta
in questa favola bella che ieri ci illuse
e oggi teneramente ci serra.

Monte Porzio, maggio 1987

For Love

We have stored our old dreams
in the basement, snuggled close,
they will keep each other company
they will tell each other tales
of our ancient splendors and sorrows
and of all the pearls we gave
to those we loved perhaps in vain.
Pictures trinkets papers and phrases:
how pathetic and odious they seem now
all jumbled together
with the scent of death in this
repetition. Gone is their fullness and nothingness
and perhaps repeating ourselves is all we know
living better
while living less.
Because everything, Rosanna, adds up
and nothing is erased. Just as the poet told
in the beautiful fable that seduced us yesterday
and clutches us tenderly today.

Monte Porzio, May 1987

Forza-mattina
scapricciato aprirsi d'un fiore
punge in viso la chiarìa marina
stringe un nuovo pensare, aurora
virgulto, spiraglio di luce, garitta
e poi boccaporto, finestra che si denuda
fuga-vigneto immenso
scena aperta un istante prima della corsa
occhi-luce: la prima parola che penso.

Monte Porzio, gennaio 1988

Morning-ardor
a flower's whimsical bloom
the skin-piercing marine lucidity
grasps a new thought, dawn
shoot, glimmer of light, sentry post
and then the passageway, the window
exposed, immense vineyard-escape
scene disclosed an instant before the race
eyes-aura: the first word in my thoughts.

Monte Porzio, January 1988

Privato scenario di precipizi
vertigine dei passaggi, finzioni, visioni
velo molle alla brezza
teoria di volti noti mascherati
neutro mistero, fiaccola, cigno
che si consuma bruciandosi in acqua
ragazzi fuggiti nella foresta
un nascondiglio per ogni perla rubata
lama fresca della notte o spina di rosa
rossa amorosa, freccia puntata
rimasta attaccata al suo arco
ecco una salita:
alla destra la vecchia casa di Fratte
a sinistra il monte Stella
corre davanti il mio cane
sangue e saliva guizza la lingua, smania
d'una ricerca spira di se stessa,
bambino, m'inerpico su per la salita
rivedo mio padre, rivedo il ponte
che ingrandisce a dismisura
cerco nei miei piccoli passi
una statura in cui riconoscermi
m'aggrappo alla fuggente vita
e già tutto si fa nostalgia
o febbrile utopia.

East Setauket, febbraio 1990

Private movie-set of cliffs,
dizzying paths, illusions, visions,
veil yielding to the breeze,
masks of famous faces in procession,
pale mystery, torch, swan
consumed by flames over water,
boys turned fugitives in the woods
a hiding place for every stolen pearl,
night's chilling blade or the thorn
of an ardent red rose, aimed arrow
poised on the bow
here's the way up:
the old house in Fratte to the right
Mount Stella to the left,
my dog runs ahead
tongue quivering with blood and saliva, frenzy
of a quest recoiling on itself
a child, I crawl the ascent,
I see my father again, see the bridge again
looming vastly large,
I search in my small steps
for a dimension in which to recognize myself,
I cling to a life that flees
and everything becomes nostalgia
or a feverish dreamery.

East Setauket, February 1990

a Francesco Paolo Memmo (I)
(come in sogno)

Doveva certo trattarsi di un gioco da ragazzi:
una palla che correva in discesa
e io che cercavo di raggiungerla
e: "fermala!", a qualcuno più in basso
che avrebbe potuto aiutarmi,
poi l'ho raggiunta... ma
s'era tutta spappolata
l'ho lanciata in avanti più che potevo
pensando (simultaneamente)
alla tanta strada che avrei dovuto rifare...
ma qui, lì, è successo qualcosa: uno scatto
uno spostamento, una sovrimpressione
di qualcosa che avveniva o era appena avvenuto
poco fa... con qualcuno che aveva chiesto
di restare con me, e di colpo
un'immagine parallela e insistente
di tanti corpi ammassati in una piccola stanza
e poi all'improvviso la visione
d'una pianta gigantesca, di questa
pianta qui, davanti a me,
che s'è fatta presenza oscura e tangibile,
fresco richiamo di vita
figura misteriosa, inevitabile.

... e dire che solo di neve avrei voluto parlare
di questa lenta bianca fioccata di stelle.

Port Jefferson, febbraio 1987

For Francesco Paolo Memmo (I)
(as in a dream)

Surely it must have been a childhood game:
a ball rolling downhill
me running after it
shouting: "Stop it!" to someone below
who could have helped,
but then I caught up to it... and
it was a soggy mess.
I threw it back as hard as I could
thinking (all the while)
of all the distance I would have to hike back,
but here, there, something occurred: a click,
a shift, a double exposure
of something happening now or just having happened
not long ago... with someone who had asked
to stay with me, and all at once
a persistent parallel image
of a heap of bodies in a tiny room
and then suddenly the apparition
of huge foliage, this plant
here before me now
that's become a tangible, obscure presence
a rousing call to life
a mysterious, inescapable figure.

… and to think I was only going to speak of the snow
of these slow white flakes of stars.

Port Jefferson, February 1987

a Francesco Paolo Memmo (II)

Ciò che resta è questa oscurità
puntuale e immutata della notte
arma sospesa che vacilla
e si frantuma di fronte ai miei sogni
o fa palizzate ai ritornati desideri
alle amene illusioni
alle mie scombinate chimere: ecco,
pensare, ad esempio, alle cose
che avresti potuto intraprendere
oggi vent'anni fa.
Perché dunque mi parli di treni
perduti, amico mio?
Si perde davvero il treno?
Per quanto mi riguarda
ci sono sempre rimasto dentro, io.

Monte Porzio, gennaio 1988

For Francesco Paolo Memmo (II)

What remains is this punctual and immutable
darkness of the night
suspended force that trembles
and shatters before my dreams
or fences off the resurgence of my desires
my comfortable illusions
my disorderly fantasies: so,
think, for example, of all the things
that you could have undertaken
today twenty years ago.
Why do you speak, then, my friend
of missed trains?
Does one really miss a train?
I for one
have always remained on board.

Monte Porzio, January 1988

Debolezza stasera

Debolezza stasera non presuppone un prima
né un dopo: è tenerezza senza referenti
una liquida incertezza che invade
l'abitacolo intero una barca
che fa acqua mollemente e mollemente
s'inabissa.

Debolezza stasera è il primo passo nella casa deserta
un'aurea leggerezza che rotea improvvisa
intorno a se stessa e ricerca gli oggetti
d'uso comune sùbito ritoccati rimessi
in funzione perché la loro plausibilità
inneschi quella dell'automa riflesso.

Debolezza stasera è qualche telefonata
agli ex e alle ex di turno
in perfetta sincronia, del resto,
al film di se stesso, interrogando il manichino
e il manicomio d'attorno, il suo gesto fermo
ambulante vagante impietrito
l'eterno recitativo, il suo sabba di sabbia. Un detrito.

Debolezza stasera è il sonno traditore
un lieve vociare di bambini
in lontananza o nel sogno
prato d'acqua in fondo al mare
piovra lenta che s'allenta
balla Shéhérazade scherza
schiuma
aria
colori.

East Setauket, marzo 1990

A Weakness Tonight

A weakness tonight assuming neither a before
nor an after: a tenderness without reference,
a fluid uncertainty pervading
the entire vessel, a boat
that's quietly leaking and quietly
sinking.

A weakness tonight marks my first step into a desolate home,
a golden lightness suddenly rotating
around itself and searching for ordinary
objects touched again and quickly put back to use
so that their existence can trigger
a reflection of reality upon this automaton.

A weakness tonight means a few phone calls
to former friends and temporary lovers,
in perfect synchrony, of course,
with the film of himself, questioning the mannequin
and madhouse all around him, his gestures firm,
wandering, roaming, dead still,
an eternal recital, his Sabbath of Sand. Rubbish.

A weakness tonight is a treacherous sleep
and the gentle calling of children
in the distance or a dream,
a watery meadow at the bottom of the sea,
a sluggish octopus sluggishly uncoiling,
dancing Shéhérazade, bewitches
seafoam
air
rainbow of colors.

East Setauket, March 1990

Ritrovarti a caso, un istante solo,
mentre cresce nell'Uovo grigio
lo sgradinato scomporsi dell'ora.

Lassù oltre il fiacco lucernario
l'albero s'arrende al vento
prima che il buio lo assorba del tutto.

Stride vicino la nota insistente
come una lama o lacrima-luna
divertita a squarciare

la stessa e la stessa ferita.
Cerco un Interiore: a chi parlo invano?
Tu dormi le mille miglia lontano.

East Setauket, 29 aprile 1990, h.19,45

To find you again by chance, if only for a moment,
while within the Gray Egg
the hour's disorderly dissolution grows.

There beyond the dim skylight
the tree surrenders to the wind
before darkness absorbs all.

Not far away the howl of insistent music
like a knife or tears of moon
delighting in the laceration of

the same, same wound.
I search for the Interior: to whom do I call out in vain?
You are sleeping a thousand miles away.

East Setauket, April 29, 1990, 7:45 p.m.

Ceres
(in treno)

Qui è nata la mia donna peruviana
occhi d'uva passita – come la descrisse un poeta –
e il viso scolpito nella pietra che sfida
queste montagne, testarda come loro
a stipare i segreti del tempo
e la grazia dei giorni
felici infelici d'infanzia.
Da lei ho appreso il lavoro delle mani
e come un giorno di sventura si trasformi
in sorriso della terra, incurante
d'ogni ambascia e di colpo svestito
d'ogni nostra atavica paura.
Terra del tempo di cui s'è nutrita la tua bocca
a volte ti penso come lontano idolo, incanto
da ritrovare di colpo intatto
dopo una manciata di giorni-anni
che in fretta, troppo in fretta, ci passano accanto.

Roma-Pescara, 28 giugno 1990

Ceres
(On the train)

My Peruvian woman was born here
raisin-eyed – as a poet described her once –
face chiseled in a stone that defies
these mountains, stubborn as they are
hoarding time's secrets
with the grace of childhood's
blissful sorrowful days.
I learned from her how to labor with my hands
and how to transform a day of misfortune
into a smile of the earth, indifferent
to all distress and suddenly stripped bare
of our most primitive fears.
Land of time that nourished you
sometimes I think of you as a distant idol
an enchantment I suddenly found intact
after a handful of days-years
that fast, too fast, pass us by.

Rome-Pescara, June 28, 1990

Neapolitan moonlight
(per Maurizio Vignola)

Teneri alla mente circonfusi
da mille direzioni occhimani
che s'accalcano alla ressa dei giorni
stracca pantomima di chi poco s'aspetta:
eppure tutto continua affabilmente
crudelmente in rima.
Come siamo superati, amico mio,
e come stortamente stonato
sembra oggi il motivo di questa
canzone: graffia malamente nelle ossa
non più giovani, mentre spiazzati
ci recitiamo addosso un'altra preghiera.
O nostre irriducibili voglie
(ingenuamente confessate l'un l'altro)
in questa bavosa serata marzolina.
Siamo rimasti un po' indietro,
bambini impreparati
al mondo che cammina.

Napoli, 11 marzo 1991

Neapolitan Moonlight
(for Maurizio Vignola)

Soothing to the mind surrounded
from all directions by eyes-hands
that crowd in on the rush of days
a listless pantomime from one who expects little:
and yet everything goes on affably,
cruelly rhyming.
How dated we've become, my friend,
how warped and twisted
seems our song's refrain today:
grating horribly into our bones
that are no longer young, displaced,
we endlessly recite prayers.
O our unrelenting desires
(confessed naïvely to each other)
in this drooling spring night.
We've remained behind the time,
children unprepared,
for a world that moves by.

Naples, March 11, 1991

a Romolo Runcini

Città di fantasmi e di frantumi
che ho percorso di notte su scuri
lastroni di pietra mentre
mi spiegavi affabilmente
storie d'intrighi un tempo guizzati
a memoria serpentina tra i fitti
e infiniti meandri sotterranei –
almeno così recitava il racconto
del fido accompagnatore – la mente
altrove e altrove girava posandosi
in angoli e spigoli, bassi e frontoni
fino improvvisamente sul volto
d'una prostituta bambina:
sostava sghemba nei pressi d'un bar
e che tu per un istante avresti voluto salvare
(salvare da cosa?), fu poi
emozionante nel sogno la proposta
d'una semplice compagnia
un'accorata conversazione, che ora
allora si sarebbe rispecchiata
in pura avventura di scrittura
o immaginaria memoria.

Napoli, 10 aprile 1987

For Romolo Runcini

City of illusions and phantoms
that I pursued at night on dark
slabs of stone while
you graciously told me
tales of intrigue a time darting
through a serpentine memory
through endless dense subterranean labyrinths
– at least as the faithful companion
told the tale – the mind elsewhere
and turning elsewhere it settled
upon corners and edges, gables and pediments
until suddenly it fell upon the face
of a child prostitute:
paused crouching over by a bar
and for a moment you had wished to save her
(save her from what?), then the dream
became more emotional
the offer of simple companionship
a mournful conversation that would now
and then be reflected
in the pure adventure of writing
or an imaginary memory.

Naples, April 10, 1987

Quattro barche di pescatori
su di un mare lattiginoso:
stenta qui la memoria a coniugare

queste immagini di repertorio
alle riaffermate urgenze dell'oggi
io disertore spento che di passaggio

(sempre di passaggio) trasferisco
duri segni di aggiornati retaggi
in immagini di vita riflessa:

è buono questo mare
è buona questa terra
per tutti i suoi figli eletti e reietti.

Napoli-Salerno, marzo 1991

Four fishing boats
on a cloudy sea:
here my memory struggles to conjoin

these commonplace images
with today's pressing needs
I a weary deserter just drifting through

(always drifting through) I transform
harsh signs of a past revisited
into images of reflected life:

this sea is good
this earth is good
to all of its chosen and exiled ones.

Naples-Salerno, March 1991

29 agosto 1954

La casa sbucava improvvisa
dopo uno stretto baratto di curve
da un lato la sua bianca facciata
dall'altro la montagnola che
giorno dopo giorno rinfocolava
i nostri impuri fuochi
o delitti mentali.
Per Elvira – m'è caro questo nome
così antiquato, qui e ora – era
facile tenerci a bada: a chi
uno svelto sorriso a chi una setolosa
promessa a chi un finto appuntamento
io poi che m'ostinavo
a offrirle la mia bicicletta.
Di più poco ricordo
e molto certo ho riposto.
Una data, però:
il primo bacio rubato per gioco
una sera dolcelunga d'agosto.

Salerno, maggio 1991

August 29, 1954

The house suddenly appeared
beyond a narrow curving bank
from one side its white facade
from the other the tiny knoll
that day after day rekindled
our unchaste fires
our crimes of thought.
For Elvira – a name so dear to me
now so quaint – it was
easy to keep us all at bay: to one,
a sly smile, to another a quick
promise, to a third a pretend rendezvous.
I was the one who then persisted
in offering her my bicycle.
I don't remember much more
and much I have certainly dismissed.
One date, however:
the first kiss stolen in a game
on a long, sweet August night.

Salerno, May 1991

Sussurrato vibrare d'un albero in piena
primavera dalla finestra aperta
d'una biancasala di conferenze
intanto che un molle relatore srotola
parola dopo parola
entrano escono si perdono nella testa
mentre l'aria cincischia circola
da un interno che vola
a un esterno che resta.

Stony Brook, 3 giugno 1991

Quivering whisper of a tree in full blossom
from the open window
of the white-walled conference hall
while a listless speaker unrolls
word after word
coming going getting lost in our thoughts
as the air dawdles and circulates
from an interior that takes flight
to an exterior that stays still.

Stony Brook, June 3, 1991

Il ramo dell'albero

Il ramo dell'albero
è una mano che si tende
verso la finestra. Vorrei
allungare la mia e
intrecciati come due adolescenti
camminare insieme per la via.

The Branch of the Tree

The branch of the tree
is a hand extended
toward my window. If only I could
outstretch mine
like two adolescents
we'd walk together arm in arm
down the road.

PAROLE PER EMMA

penso a un piccolo elefante
appeso a un pallone a forma
di cuore che rideva nell'aria
al di là del precipizio
a chi s'era fermato
proprio nei pressi dell'orlo
senza osare il salto nel

C'è tanto rosa oggi qui attorno
niente ci può separare

Stanzas for Emma

I think of a baby elephant
hanging from a heart-shaped balloon
in the air
over the abyss
laughing at those who halted
at the edge
without daring to leap...

There's so much pink around today
nothing can come between us.

I

La notte qualcuno al mio posto
si alza più di una volta
siccome vedo perfettamente nel buio
gli do istruzioni senza parlargli
perché eviti scontri coi mobili
o con aguzze sporgenze.
Lui si muove lentamente
strusciando lieve i piedi per terra
evita la cassapanca dopo averne
tastato il legno della bordatura, sfiora
il grande armadio con le dita,
ecco lo spigolo del comò
la fugace carezza all'antiquata crespina
la falsa canadella il vecchio vaso di vetro
coi fiori secchi d'acetosella, la culla di Emma, e poi e poi.
E poi ritornando al suo posto si dissolve
buio nel buio
nero nel nero più cupo.

Monte Porzio, gennaio 1988

I

Someone else takes my place at night
arising time after time
since I can see perfectly in the dark
I silently guide him
to avoid bumping into furniture
or sharp corners.
He moves slowly
lightly shuffling his feet over the floor
he misses the toy chest having tapped
against its wooden trim, lightly touches
the armoire with his fingertips,
here's the edge of the dresser
a passing caress of the ceramic bowl
the imitation antique pitcher the old glass vase
with its dried sorrel flowers, Emma's cradle, and then, and then.
And then returning to his place he fades away
dark into dark
black into deepest black.

Monte Porzio, January 1988

II

Emma che ride alla gaia ebbrezza
profumo di violetta sprizza
nell'aria con fiabe e ginestra
ora incantata carillon saetta
al tuo sorriso, svelta
movenza di manine, mentre
ti guardo sempre più smarrito e
stupito di questa tua *innocente esattezza.*

Monte Porzio, gennaio 1988

II

Laughing, with a giddy intoxication,
Emma is spraying the air with violet scents
tinged with broom and fairy tales
now the enchanted carillon dances
to your smile, a swift
motion of little hands, while
I watch you ever more bewildered
and amazed by your *innocent precision.*

Monte Porzio, January 1988

III

Vai scoprendo lo specchio:
se ti ci porto davanti
ti guardi incantata, quasi stupita
tendi la mano all'altra te stessa
per afferrarla.
Altre volte vorresti azzannarla.
Altre volte, se troppo ti ci avvicino,
te ne ritrai per paura o fastidio
o rifiuto d'eccessivo contatto.
O che altro?

Monte Porzio, luglio 1988

III

You're discovering mirrors:
If I bring you up to the glass,
you watch yourself amazed and mesmerized
you stretch out your hand to grasp
your other self.
Sometimes you try to bite her.
Sometimes, if I take you up too close,
you pull back out of fear or frustration
or rejection of so much contact.
Or what else?

Monte Porzio, July 1988

IV

Stamattina t'ho vista che cercavi
ripetutamente d'afferrare l'acqua
con le tue piccole mani
ma non ci riesci a possedere
quell'asticciola liquida e trasparente
non ci riesci
e rifletti pensosa, forse rifletti
– ma è solo un momento –
sull'impossibilità d'afferrarla
forse ti sembra assurdo che (già) esista
un divieto, o qualcosa d'inaccessibile,
tu che tocchi con mano ogni tuo sogno
ogni mio sogno
e fai di qualunque utopia
la tua grande concreta innocente
Realtà.

Monte Porzio, agosto 1988

IV

This morning I saw you persistently
trying to grasp the water
with your little hands
but you can't hold onto
that translucent, liquid shaft
you can't
and just for a moment you pensively reflect,
perhaps reflect
upon the impossibility of ever grasping it
maybe it seems absurd that (already)
a prohibition exists, something inaccessible,
to you who touch with your hands your every dream
my every dream
and transform any fantasy
into your great innocent tangible
Reality.

Monte Porzio, August 1988

V

Sempre rapido e poco
il tempo
nei tuoi occhi rapiti
volti e figure s'avvicendano
senza suddivisione
tanto che tu riassumi
in un lampo
chi mancava da giorni.

Monte Porzio, agosto 1988

V

Time
swift and brief
in your spellbound eyes
faces and shapes alternate
seamlessly
so that you reabsorb
in a flash
someone gone for days.

Monte Porzio, August 1988

Abissi del tempo
calmezza di larghi orizzonti
i tuoi occhi
di serra calamita d'acqua
aria fuggita per sempre
da fitte barriere di spine.
C'è un angelo Rosa...
che veglia terreno su te:
è di radica buona, radice
forte e benigna in te radicata.
Sei come lei grande, verde e serena.

Monte Porzio, agosto 1988

VI

Voids of time
serenity of broad horizons
your eyes
a greenhouse a water magnet
the air forever freed
from dense barricades of thorns
There's an angel on earth, a Rose...
who watches over you:
she comes from good stock, her strong
benevolent roots are rooted in you
You who resemble her: grand, green, and serene.

Monte Porzio, August 1988

VII

Guardo la tua piccola nuca mentre
spingo il carrozzino per qualche giro
che insieme facciamo. Non ci parliamo,
anche volendo – certo volendo – non
potremmo. Le nostre comunicazioni
si riducono a sorrisi, gesti, moine,
ammiccamenti e pochi altri armeggiamenti.
Guardo la tua piccola nuca piena di riccioli
sparsi che si volta ora di qua ora di là
nella millimetrica scoperta
dell'Universo *che incontro ti viene.*
Io non saprò mai spiegarti
di che disperata allegrezza è fatta questa
pura visione dei tuoi riccioli al vento
di questa tua nuchina che s'inoltra
e s'inoltra
in tutta la sua sconvolgente innocenza
nel folto del mondo e a petto d'ogni
Malanno, oggi, soprattutto oggi,
festa del tuo compleanno.

Monte Porzio, 4 ottobre 1988

VII

My eyes fall to the tiny nape of your neck
as I take you out for a stroll
in the baby carriage. We say nothing
though wanting to – certainly wanting to –
but we can't. Our communication
is reduced to smiles and hugs, winks,
gestures and other such inventions.
My eyes fall to your tiny nape full of curls
strewn here and there
in the discovery of the Universe
that slowly *inches towards you.*
I will never know how to explain to you
the desperate joy that comes from
this pure vision of your curls in the wind
of your tiny little nape that nudges ahead
further ahead
in all its unsettling innocence
into the thick of the world into the bosom of
every Evil, today, especially today
on the celebration of your birthday.

Monte Porzio, October 4, 1988

VIII

A quest'ora stai dormendo
ignara del grido squarcio
lanciato dietro di me dentro di me:
m'ha seguito come un cane ferito
per tutta la durata del viaggio.

Salerno, 5 marzo 1989

VIII

You're sleeping by now
unaware of the cry, the laceration
hurled behind me inside me:
like a wounded dog it has followed me
throughout the journey.

Salerno, March 5, 1989

IX

Tu ancora non lo sai
né pensarci puoi, ma sappi
che tutto si può immaginare
a questo mondo. Basta volerlo
e il polo nord diventa il polo sud
e se vuoi
puoi d'improvviso volare
o vivere nell'acqua, e attraversare
il fuoco come niente
o pensare di afferrare dal cielo
la bella più Stella.
Poi resta tutto come prima
ma intanto
hai pensato una cosa straordinaria:
grazie a quel girotondo
sei diventata più forte
vera padrona di te stessa e del mondo.

Monte Porzio, aprile 1989

IX

You don't know it yet,
nor can you intend it, but be aware
that everything in this world
can be imagined. Just make a wish
and the North Pole becomes the South Pole
and if you want to
you can suddenly fly
or live under water, or walk through
fire like nothing
or think of grasping the clearest star of Stars
from the sky.
Then everything is as before
but meanwhile
you have contemplated something extraordinary:
thanks to that ring around the roses
you have become empowered
the true mistress of yourself and the world.

Monte Porzio, April 1989

X

Potessi spiegarti
quel tuo terso apparire
che mi regali ogni volta...
    Sprizza
di colpo nell'aria
e ogni cosa contagia
giratrottola in ogni direzione
trillo sorriso brilla tumultuoso
e dilaga nella stanza
mentre io estasiato assetato di te m'alimento
di te mi riempio
e bevo a somiglianza e
m'apparento al tuo giocatempo.

Monte Porzio, aprile 1989

X

If I could just describe
that lucent appearance
that you offer to me each time...
                    It surges
suddenly into the air
imprinting everything
a top spinning in all directions
fluttering sound tumultuous smile that shines
and flows into the room
while ecstatic I thirst for you am nourished
by you I fill up
and drink in your likeness
and am united in your timeplay.

Monte Porzio, April 1989

XI

Un treno arriva lento alla stazione
infila il binario morto e si ferma
il poeta vi sale e s'addormenta.

Ecco allora che il treno si rimuove
se ne parte con il poeta dentro
parte per un paese nuovo e antico

il paese dei giochi e dei balocchi
laggiù il tempo si ripete contento
e tutti i calendari hanno lo stesso

giorno. In quel mondo è tutto un girotondo
d'alberi infiorati fresche rosade
i gridi dei bambini nelle strade

trilli di merli fughe di rondoni
lì servi non ci trovi né padroni
tutto avviene in un solo accadimento.

Io vorrei tanto andarci un giorno con te
per starvi contento senza pensiero
stordito gaio e solo di te fiero

bambino anch'io portato per mano
da te piano piano in quel grande regno
ove sogno e memoria colorano il vento.

Monte Porzio, aprile 1989

XI

A train slowly pulls into the station,
and stops at the track's dead end.
The poet gets on and falls asleep.

And then the train starts to move again
taking off with the poet aboard
departing for a new and ancient land

the land of games and toys
where time happily repeats itself
and all calendars display the same day

In that world everything's a ring around the roses
of flowering trees and fresh rose beds
cries of children in the streets

trills of blackbirds flights of swallows
there neither servants nor masters you'll find
everything happens at once

I wish I could go there someday with you
to remain content without a worry
amazed light-hearted simply proud of you

I become a child too taken by your hand
ever so slowly into the great kingdom
where dream and memory color the wind.

Monte Porzio, April 1989

XII

Una matita piena di stelle, Emma,
per disegnare un sogno che si perde,
poterti dire sempre e solo l'oggi
quanto più mi sforzo a ri-tenerlo
tale quale nei miei pensieri
ché, vedi, *con te più non distinguo ieri da ieri.*

East Setauket, ottobre 1989

XII

Emma, a star-laden pencil
to sketch a vanishing dream
to speak to you forever and only of today
I strive all the more to hold onto it
exactly as in my thoughts
since, you see, when I am with you,
I can no longer tell yesterday from yesterday.

East Setauket, October 1989

XIII
(da una foto)

T'investe una molle luce pomeridiana
su questo letto
caldo di sospiri e di gioie agrette
da cui sprizzasti un giorno folgorante.
Hai riposto accanto
e forse anche scordato per un istante
il tuo giochetto
e mi guardi serena e fiduciosa
ch'io più non riparta per strade
lontane insidiose accidiose.
A te basta impietrirmi con i tuoi occhi sani
e la piccola mano
ferma
sulla mia valigia.

East Setauket, ottobre 1989

XIII
(from a photograph)

A supple afternoon light envelops you
on this bed
warm with sighs and the soursweet joys
from which you burst one dazzling day.
You set aside
and perhaps for a while even forgot
your little toy
and you look at me calmly trusting
that I won't take off ever again
for dangerous distant indolent roads.

For you it's enough to turn me to stone
with your innocent eyes
and your tiny hand
firm and still
on my suitcase.

East Setauket, October 1989

XIV

All'aria tutto il cartame catrame
    una volta per tutte
volare e non volere
che sia avere uguale ad essere
senza scuse o ritardi o infingimenti.
Con te soltanto
nel mondo-modo che vorresti
e che vorrei
ma anche tu, bambina mia,
ci lascerai.

East Setauket, 6 novembre 1989

XIV

All this paper all this tar
up in the air once and for all,
to fly rather than to wish
to have the same as to be
with no excuses, delays or disguises.
With you alone
in the world-way that you
and I wish for
but even you, my child,
will leave us.

East Setauket, November 6, 1989

XV
(Trasposizioni)

D'un limitato potere d'intervento
azioni finzioni, effetti diversi
quando cause esterne s'affacciano
al di là del nostro prevedibile
come ieri dinanzi a quel calciatore
che s'accasciò improvvisamente sul campo
senza un grido o un'espressione
di richiamo...

Dire d'un ripetersi
e d'un ritornare, d'un cancellare
e d'un ricominciare, scordare
con un colpo di spugna
come se da capo
un semplice inizio di calendario
corrispondesse a nuove configurazioni
del vedersi e del vedere.

Cancellarmi nel tuo gioco, Emma,
l'infinita geografia che trabocca
da quel fazzoletto di stoffa su cui sei seduta
spiarti le mosse e
i tuoi infingimenti reali
trasposizioni senza passato
e senza futuro.

Scomparsa ogni domanda:
il palloncino è volato dalla finestra
e ormai sale in alto senza legami.
Siamo rimasti insieme a guardarlo
fino a che è stato possibile
come per quest'anno che tra poco se ne andrà

XV
(Transpositions)

Actions, pretences, varied effects –
a limited power of intervention
when external causes appear
that we could not predict
like facing that soccer player yesterday
who collapsed suddenly on the field
without a cry or a gesture of
appeal...

To speak of repetition
and return, an obliteration
and a new start, to wipe from memory
with the swipe of a sponge
as if commencing anew as if
a calendar's modest beginning
corresponded with new dimensions
of envisioning and envisioning oneself.

To lose myself in your game, Emma,
in the infinite geography that overflows
from the patch of fabric on which you sit
to spy on your moves and
ingenuous imitations
transpositions without past
or future.

All questions vanished:
the tiny balloon sailed through the window
and now soars up free of all ties.
We stayed there watching it together
as long as we could
the same as for this year that soon will pass

perché così dice l'ultimo foglio
rimasto appeso sul muro.

Ma tu mi guardi
e mi solleciti ad afferrarlo quel palloncino
m'investi d'un potere d'intervento
che non puoi mettere in dubbio.
Hai ragione. Tutto è possibile,
tutto scompare dinanzi a questo
tuo viso terso, a questo tuo dito
sperso che indica in alto nell'aria,
dinanzi al tuo riso mazzolino di stelle
filanti che accendo senza posa.
E io non penso più al conto corteo dei giorni
la vita è una sola tenerezza
una trasposizione, un vento
in un Tuttopresente,
ed io vivo la mia infinita giovinezza.

Monte Porzio, 31 dicembre 1989 - 1 gennaio 1990

because the last sheet of the calendar
tacked on the wall says so.
But you look at me
and implore me to catch that tiny balloon
you invest me with a power of intervention
that you cannot doubt.
You're right. All is possible,
everything disappears in front of your
clear face, your loose finger
pointing high into the air,
in front of your laughter, that little bundle
of shooting stars that I continue to ignite.
And I think no more of the sums and series of days
life is a tender unity
a transposition, a passing breeze
in an All-present
where I live my infinite youth.

Monte Porzio, December 31, 1989 - January 1, 1990

XVI

Mi fanno compagnia sera e mattino
proprio accanto al mio letto
una palla un caleidoscopio un trenino:
tre giocattoli che ho conservato per te
pronti al mio prossimo viaggio.
Un curioso decoro:
prime e ultime cose che scorgo,
scriccia pepita,
all'aprire e al chiudere degli occhi.
Vedi come grazie a loro
salto viaggio impasto la vita.

East Setauket, maggio 1990

XVI

Night and day they keep me company
right by my bed
a ball a kaleidoscope a tiny train:
three toys that I've kept for you
ready for my next trip.
An odd decor
the first and last things I notice,
a tiny little nugget,
for me to open and close my eyes to.
See, thanks to them,
I bounce back I travel I knit my life together.

East Setauket, May 1990

XVII

Penso stasera a quei bianchi cavalli
che popolavano le mie piccole storie
nel buio vicino al mio letto
a quei trenini d'un finto Far West
alle steppe deserte alle rigogliose savane
a Nemo e ai figli del capitano Grant
ai tesori nascosti in quelle isole
che poi regolarmente s'inabbissavano
dopo un tremendo boato. Nel sogno
un vento li spinge lontano
un suono di flauto
riga un'aria sgomenta
i miei cento colori
in un solo deserto. All'improvviso
fa freddo, e da qui ogni altro confine
è perso o incerto.

East Setauket, maggio 1990

XVII

Tonight I think of those white horses
that filled my childhood tales
in the dark next to my bed
of those toy trains from a make-believe Wild West
of the desert steppes, of the lush savannas
of Nemo and the sons of Captain Grant
of the hidden treasures on those islands
that would inevitably always sink
after a terrible roar. In my dreams
a great wind blows them afar
the sound of a flute
outlines an enchanted tune
my hundreds of colors
in one desert alone. Suddenly
it turns cold and from here all borders are
lost or uncertain.

East Setauket, May 1990

XVIII

L'uccellino che l'estate scorsa
tenesti per gioco nelle tue mani
stamattina è venuto fin qui:
l'ho scorto ad un tratto dalla finestra
beccava tra i fili d'erba
e mi parlava di te.
Ho rivisto la foto di quella
strepitosa mattina
la tua aria svagata incantata
la mia gioia di padre bambino smarrito,
candida gemma, mio Sogno infinito.

East Setauket, maggio 1990

XVIII

The little bird you held
in your hand for fun last summer
flew back to us this morning:
from the window I suddenly spied him
pecking at the blades of grass
telling me all about you.
I have seen the photograph of
that glorious morning once again
your enchanted dreamy air
the joy a childlike father lost
pure gemstone, my infinite Dream.

East Setauket, May 1990

XIX

Il sole la luna le stelle
le belle figure di questa
disarmata contrada
te le regalo tutte
in questo fazzoletto festoso
dove stamani nuotano il Gialloro
e il Verdesospiroso.
Sorride la prima figura: è
sicura, non ha bisogno
d'altra forza, serrata aperta
nella sua regale corona. La seconda
sottostante è un po' sardonica
vigilante: ha perso la corona
vagola nuda diletta graziosa.
Ma la più bella è quella
che raggia sulla tua fronte
di tutte madre o sorella maggiore,
mai non si tace, vibra
infinita, scapriola
facendosi beffa d'ogni parola.
Intride un ultimo sussurro: invita
alla vita.

Montesilvano-Monte Porzio, luglio/agosto 1990

XIX

Sun moon stars
the beautiful figures of this
tender land
I give them all to you
in this scarf of celebration
where this morning the Gilded-Yellow
and the Sighing-Green bathe.
The first figure smiles:
confident, it has no need
of external sustenance, locked open
in its regal crown. Further down,
the second one is mildly ironic,
cautious: it has lost its crown
and meanders naked beloved gracious.
But most beautiful is the one
shining from your forehead
a mother or older sister of all
never silent, it pulses
infinite, it leaps
making fun of every word.
It inspires in a whisper: an invitation
to live.

Montesilvano-Monte Porzio, July/August 1990

XX

. . . .
bastava lo scricchiolio della scala di ferro
a svegliarti e a farti immediatamente
capire che uno di noi due ti stava
lasciando o raggiungendo, piccola rosa...

East Setauket, 30 gennaio 1991

XX

. . . .
the creak of the metal stairs was enough
to wake you and to make you instantly
understand that one of us was
leaving or joining you, little rose...

East Setauket, January 30, 1991

XXI

(*per anarrosi*)

Stamattina come svuotato
di qualsiasi spinta
poco fa una breve passeggiata con la Scriccia
ancora convalescente per la bronchitaccia
dei giorni scorsi
il figlio d'Amerigo è venuto
a tagliare l'erbaccia
(lo sta ancora facendo):
la falciatrice elettrica mi buca(va) la testa
(magari la falciasse magari)
sul ciglio della strada
abbiamo raccolto fiori di camomilla
"perché?" ha chiesto Emma,
poi ha voluto per forza aiutarmi
a sistemarli nella ciotola
che abbiamo lasciato all'aperto.
Li faremo essiccare,
forse li useremo il prossimo inverno.

Monte Porzio, 11 giugno 1991

XXI
(*listlessly*)

This morning – drained
of all drive – I took
a stroll with my little Squirrel a while ago
still recovering over the past few days
from bronchitis.
Amerigo's son has come
to cut the weeds
(he's still working at it).
The electric lawnmower drilling/drilled through my head
(if only it could mow everything down).
We picked chamomile flowers
at the edge of the road.
Emma asked, "Why?"
and then helped me insistently
to arrange them in the bowl
that we left outside.
We decide to let them dry,
perhaps for use next winter.

Monte Porzio, June 11, 1991

XXII
(*per il quarto compleanno*)

Fra un po' ti vedrò spuntare
palletta leggera e volante come un
fringuello accecato di luce e di gioia.

Lo vedrò spiccare il volo tra la gente
e nessuno e niente potrà misurare
quell'attimo-luce che ci distanzia.

Ma fra te che corri verso le mie braccia
e io che ti aspetto, sono io che
t'ho già raggiunto per primo

e sto già correndo in te abbracciato
verso la figura dell'altro me stesso
di noi perdutamente innamorato.

N.Y.-Roma (nell'imminenza dell'atterraggio), 4 ottobre 1991

XXII
(For her fourth birthday)

Soon I will see you appear
my little light ball in flight
a goldfinch blinded by joy and light.

I will see it fly up through the crowd
and no one and nothing could measure
that spark-of-light that sets us apart.

But between you running into my arms
and me awaiting you, I am the first
to have reached you

and embraced by you I am already racing
towards the image of my other self
so hopelessly in love with our being together.

N.Y.-Rome (landing), October 4, 1991

XXIII
(da Vasco Graca Moura)

Sono migrati altrove gli uccelli
li ho a lungo inseguiti con gli occhi
senza seguirli
ne conservo già ogni minima traccia.
Ora fa buio più presto
il tempo non si ruba
sgocciola come il freddo per la camicia
fin dentro la pelle.

Sono migrati altrove gli uccelli
con calma saggezza
io resto qui di guardia
al nostro piccolo specchio d'acqua
su cui si son riflessi i loro stormi
e su cui tu ti sporgerai fra breve
con il tuo grandioso lacerante stupore.

Monte Porzio, ottobre 1991

XXIII
(After Vasco Graca Moura)

The birds have migrated away
for a long time my gaze followed them
without keeping track of them
I hold their faintest trace.
Darkness falls sooner now
time isn't stolen
it seeps like cold through your shirt
all the way into your skin.

The birds have migrated away
with a calm wisdom
I stand guard here
near our little mirror of water
where their flight is reflected
and where you will appear before long
with your grand wonder that tears all asunder.

Monte Porzio, October 1991

XXIV

È soprattutto quando dormi
che sciogli il drago dei tuoi cinque anni...
ah, quel filo d'erba innamorato del Sole
e dell'Ombra!
      Supina
la virente che stringi nella mano
Giostra cede il passo a Narciso
addormentato.
     L'arciere è scomparso
e a terra son rimaste le sue frecce...

Monte Porzio, ottobre 1992

XXIV

Above all it is when you sleep
that you set the dragon of your five years free...
oh, that blade of grass in love with the Sun
and the Shade!
        Supine,
the verdant Carousel that you hold in your hand
gives way to a dreaming
Narcissus.
        The archer has vanished
his arrows scattered on the ground...

Monte Porzio, October 1992

XXV

Già alla tua età – lo ricordo benissimo –
amavo la vibrante chiaría degli ulivi
di lassù se ne vedevano a centinaia
nella sonnolenza pomeridiana
d'infinite estati salernitane
qualche spillo d'ombra
una giostra incantata
nella lucentezza colorata.
Che altro donarti ora, figlia mia?
A che altro soffrire nella cupezza
di questa giornata stracca e forastica
che non accenna a finire? Infine
si fa tardi nella sera.
Una sera come un'altra.

Coram, ottobre 1992

XXV

By your age – I remember it well –
I already loved the vibrant translucence of olive trees
you could take in hundreds of them from that lookout
in the afternoon dazzle
of infinite Salerno summers
a few pinpoints of shade
an enchanted carousel
in a rainbow of radiance.
What else, my daughter, could I give you now?
What else to suffer for in the dimness
of this worn and alien day
that refuses to end? Finally,
night is falling.
A night like any other.

Coram, October 1992

XXVI

Che aria smargiassa hai in questa foto
di appenna un anno fa, mani in tasca
e berretto alla Gavroche: ne aveva uno?
l'avesse avuto sarebbe stato come il tuo
e le bretelline poi
due piccole piste su cui corrono
vertiginosamente avanti e indietro
le scolte dei tuoi quattr'anni.
Mi guardi, non mi guardi,
accenni forse a un sorriso
che vago rimescola soddisfazione
e coscienza dell'attesa.
Uscissi dal riquadro e cominciassi
a trafficarmi intorno
non ne sarei sorpreso
"su, dai, papà, vieni a giocare di là?"

Coram, dicembre 1992

XXVI

How smug you look in this photo
taken just a year ago, hands in your pockets
and a Gavroche beret: did he really wear one?
(if he did, it would have been like yours)
and those tiny suspenders
two little tracks where back and forth
at frantic speed
the guardians of your four years run.
You're looking at me, or maybe not,
perhaps a faint smile
that vaguely mixes satisfaction
with a conscious expectation.
I wouldn't be surprised if
you were to leave the picture and begin
scurrying around me.
"Come on, papa, will you play with me?"

Coram, December 1992

ARS POETICA

La sorpresa e la successiva
coscienza d'un pensare intrecciato
che fa i conti con la lentezza
di un suo voler diventare dettato:
è in questo la nostra perdita vile
tra ciò che si pensa e ciò che si scrive.

ARS POETICA

The surprise and subsequent awareness
of a woven thought
that reckons with the slowness
of its will to become written text:
in this is our vile loss
the breach between our thoughts and written words.

C'è il vedere
e tutto ciò che d'invisibiìe
si può immaginare
dunque partendo e finendo
sempre da una forma
un modello una sagoma un profilo
come seguendo le orme
d'un Mostro inafferrabile
che mi preda la notte
e scompare al mattino.

New York, febbario 1987

There's the visible
and the infinite invisible
to be imagined
thus straying from and always
resolving in a form
a pattern an outline a silhouette
like following traces
of an elusive Demon
that hunts me down by night
and disappears by morn.

New York, February 1987

Parola lino di broccato
vasta scienza in agguato
            pianura
e rivestimento d'un artificio
oltre ogni limite fisso
            oltre ogni steccato
ago di luce
affossato nel gioco dell'abisso.

New York, febbraio 1987

Words of linen and brocade
vast science waiting in ambush
          the valley
lining of artifice
beyond every intended limit
          beyond every fence
needle of light
submerged in the play of the abyss.

New York, February 1987

Nella rilettura c'è il tuffo
all'indietro di tanti momenti-alcova
la ricostruzione esatta e diversa
d'una geografia interna
pronta a slittare altrove, infiniti
ripostigli che si riaprono allo sguardo
rapito di vecchio bambino, un riposo
prolungato si anima di colpo
a nuove avventure: così
tutto ricomincia a parlare
in un tempo che imita se stesso.
Allora la morte è davvero solo un
accidente, un pretesto.

Monte Porzio, marzo 1987

Re-reading is a dive backwards
into so many cloistered moments
a precise yet altered reshaping
of an internal geography
eager to glide elsewhere, infinite
compartments that open to the entranced
gaze of an aged child, an extended
sleep that suddenly awakes
to new adventures: thus
everything starts to speak again
in a time that mimics itself.
And so death is really
only an incident, a pretext.

Monte Porzio, March 1987

a Pier Paolo Pasolini
(in memoriam)

Nell'attesa ho fatto più presto io
a scribacchiare una poesia
che lei ad arrivare.
Dunque l'attesa ha fornito il pretesto
o la pretesa di qualcosa
che rendesse meno doloroso l'aspettare
schermandone la primitiva motivazione.
Ecco, Pier Paolo, come la poesia
può davvero avere un fine pratico
un'azione, un'irriducibile manìa
o un'infinita regressione.

New York, gennaio 1986

For Pier Paolo Pasolini

Waiting, I scribbled down a poem
quicker than it took
for her to arrive.
Thus the wait furnished the pretext
or the pretense of something
that would make the waiting less painful
veiling its primal motivation.
That's how, Pier Paolo, poetry
can have a practical aim –
an action, a relentless obsession
an infinite regression.

New York, January 1986

Quando ad un tratto si fa strada in luce
virginiana tra false pastorali e soavità
di visi ignoti. Stanotte ronzava

perfetta in forma e sequenza. Che restasse
accanto n'ero certo, ma svanita è già
stamattina. Ricercarne ora il contorno

la figura, l'ombra, una marginale
rassomiglianza, almeno quella folgore
iniziale, una movenza, una parola sola,

un niente che riaccenda il perduto sogno
cui ora invano m'inchino. Pesta poesia,
innamorata del tuo manichino.

Charlottesville, aprile 1990 - East Setauket, aprile 1992

When suddenly in this Virginian light she makes her way
amidst false pastorals and sweet
unknown faces. Last night she was humming

in perfect form and sequence. Surely she would stay
by my side, I thought, but by this morning
she was gone. To search for her profile now

her shape, a shadow, a trace
of resemblance, just that first flash,
a movement, a single word,

a void to rekindle the lost dream
I surrender to now in vain. Battered poetry,
in love with your own mannequin.

Charlottesville, April 1990 – East Setauket, April 1992

a Achille Serrao
(via Landolfi)

D'un caldo afrore si compiaceva
tutta la campagna (e compagnia) attorno:
inospite e ingannevole a chi, come noi,
voleva un po' pretenziosamente
scovarne il battito segreto
come già aveva fatto
quel Solitario Abitatore... del resto.
Volevamo, caro Achille, scoprirne i passi
la visione interna esterna,
perfino il *suo* giardino: teatro
di tanti infingimenti e visionarie
costruzioni. Ma ciò che si è perso
è perso, e più non ritorna se non
in altrettanti camuffamenti o supposizioni,
vedi, come adesso. Dunque
l'unica verità fu il nome e cognome
con le date di nascita e di morte
che trovammo incise sulla sua lapide, nuda
d'ogni orpello o altro ornamento... lassù
dove l'amaro dell'alloro si fa
non già profumo, ma sentimento.

Pico Farnese-Monte Porzio, 16 agosto 1987

For Achille Serrao
(after Landofi)

The surrounding countryside (and our companions)
took delight in the hot stench:
hostile and deceptive to those like us
who wanted, perhaps a little ambitiously,
to unveil its secret heartbeat
as that Solitary Dweller...
had done before.
We wanted, my dear Achille, to trace his footsteps
the external internal vision
even *his* garden: theater
of so many simulations and visionary
constructs. But that which is lost
is lost, and returns no more, except
in many guises or conjectures,
as you see now. So
the only truths were his first and last name
and the dates of his birth and death
that we found engraved on his tombstone, devoid
of any decoration or other ornamentation... there
where the bitterness of the laurel turns
not to scent, but to sentiment.

Pico Farnese – Monte Porzio, August 16, 1987

Resistere al presente
(*via Michel Deguy*)

Poesia è nella Figura che
batte alla porta e muore sulla soglia
ascoltando il vedere
   la manifestazione
che mostra il suo niente.
Niente è evidente per sé
se non ciò che appare.
Non è sola ma danza con
la ronda delle sue accompagnatrici
apre la circostanza di un *di là*
come estensione alle
possibilità infinite del mondo
many comings all together.
Le cose non sono più oggetti né concetti
sono casi-unità
pure virtualità.

2.
Teologia della grazia e della pratica
il nascosto diventa il paragonato
parabolicamente e analogicamente
discussione e disputa
profanazione che dispiega
la rivelabilità dell'esperienza
nella teoria dei calchi
in altri modi e mezzi.
Ah, Onnipotenza paralizzata in se stessa!

Resisting Time Present
(after Michel Deguy)

1.
Poetry is the Figure
who knocks at the gate and dies on the doorstep
listening to the visible
        to the proof
that manifests her nothingness.
Nothing is self-evident
except what appears.
She does not dance alone but
with the night-watch of her companions
opening up the chance of a *beyond*
as an extension to the
infinite possibilities of the world
the many comings all together.
Objects or concepts are no longer
but instances-totality
pure virtuality.

2.
Theology of grace and practice
the hidden becomes the compared
through parable and analogy
discussion and argument
profanation that discloses
experience's potential to be revealed
through the theory of forms
and other modes and means.
Oh, omnipotence paralyzed within itself!

3.

Proporzionare cosa a cosa
– e con che mezzo –
perché l'opera artefatto microscopico
si compari con il tutto
parte del tutto di cui dà prova
labirinto che ti cresce addosso
da cui si esce per dove si è entrati.

Fuori e dentro dunque
per il dentro del dentro
per quel tutto e per quel niente.
Resistere sempre al presente.

3.
To adjust one thing to another
– and to determine how –
so that the work the microscopic artifact
can be compared to the whole
part of the whole that it documents
the labyrinth that envelops you
your exit and your entrance.
Without and within then
through inner ring within inner ring
through eternity and nothingness.
Always resisting time present.

Vibra la pagina bianca
in quest'aria autunnale
   foglia su foglia
che sopra vi scende
   come l'albero si spoglia
la pagina si riempie.

Coram, novembre 1992

The blank page quivers
in the autumnal air
        leaf after leaf
falling from above
        as the tree turns bare
the page grows full.

Coram, November 1992

BALLATE E CANZONI

Vorrei toccare una poesia
che solo sia tersa e leggera
una ballatetta una frottola una fola
una carola o tiritera, un ricciolo d'Emma
dove e ritmo e significato si facciano
unica cosa casa di vetro
illuminata dal giorno
che si sposti volando
su ogni anfratto del mondo.
Vorrei che il verso diventi universo
e che ogni cosa ritrovi il suo posto.

BALLADS AND SONGS

I wish that I could touch a poem
that's light and pure,
a little ballad, a refrain, a fairy tale,
a carol or jingle, one of Emma's curls
where sound and sense become
as one a house of glass
illuminated by day,
it would wander flying
over every chasm of the world.
I wish my verse could become a universe
and everything would find its place again.

Canzone per Paolo Conte

Stanotte il tempo è un ballerino stanco
mascherato fischietta da un molo deserto.

Un fischio che si ripete ossessivo, mentre
sbiadisce nella nebbia l'ultimo sguardo d'amore

i miei pensieri scasati, i ricordi...
profili sballati oscuri, lontane scogliere.

Non ci sarà un'altra alba, anima mia,
la sagoma di questa finestra
aperta alla notte parla di consumate allegrie
visioni smorzate laghi fermi
vecchie malattie inscatolate.

Passano davanti ai vetri
le stagioni incrociate, le stagioni
che il vento disperde...
gli antichi sorrisi di donne dietro le porte
i loro sguardi ad obliquo
mentre un bambino
spingeva correndo il suo cerchio oltre la curva...

Stanotte il tempo è un ballerino stanco.

New York, marzo-aprile 1988

Song for Paolo Conte

Tonight time is a weary dancer
shrouded, he whistles from a deserted pier.

His whistle obsessively repeated while
love's parting glance fades into mist

my thoughts, homeless, my memories...
deranged dark silhouettes, distant reefs.

My soul, you won't see another dawn,
the aperture of this window,
open to the night, speaks of worn pleasures
dimmed visions still lakes
old maladies preserved in tin.

Beyond the window panes
crisscrossed seasons pass, seasons
strewn by the wind...
the primeval smiles of cloistered women
their sideways glances
while a child, running,
spins his hoop around the bend.

Tonight time is a weary dancer.

New York, March-April 1988

Chimera
(omaggio a M. Luzi, via A. Delfini)

Ti rivedo e so ormai da che armature
ti profili, Regina adolescente,
in sparsi trasalimenti, tradimenti
che ancora riverberi.
Se talvolta la sera vacillo
di nuovo per me riconquisti il torrente del cuore
ed io ti sogno in guadi che accarezzo
per un solo momento.
Così ti lusinga chi beffa invano il riso
smorzato degli angeli di giovinezza.
Ci travolge presente assente la mente
oltre il velario, il consueto brusìo del giorno
mentre sbandano i voli nel fuoco
che certo stanotte arderà di nuovo.
Così trionfi. Così t'erigi lampeggiante
sullo specchio nero, più dell'istante
che sfavilla a occhi aperti
in un vortice di fughe. Così trionfi,
e più non sei. Né ritrovarti
posso in un cunicolo per accucciarmi
riposare, e infine parlare, parlarsi.
Perché chi si è perduto non si ferma
e più non può fermarsi.

Monte Porzio, 20 agosto 1988

Chimera
(after A. Delfini)

Queen of adolescence, I see you again
and know you by your armored profile,
strewn steps, betrayals
that you still echo.
If sometimes at night I waver
you conquer anew the torrent of my heart
and I dream of you crossing over seas
that for a moment I caress.
This is how the one who vainly mocks
the muffled laughter of angels of youth
deceives you.
Present absent the mind transports us
beyond the veil, the daily buzz
while flights swerve into the fire
that tonight will surely blaze anew.
This is how you triumph. This is how you rise up
flashing in the black mirror, glittering
extending the moment that shimmers wide-eyed
within a whirlpool of trajectories. This is how you triumph
and then you're gone. Nor can I find you again
to curl into a comforting shelter
and speak at last, speak to each other.
Because he who is lost cannot stop moving
and can never stop moving again.

Monte Porzio, August 20, 1988

Canzonetta

C'è stato un tempo in cui scrivevo
con una penna a inchiostro verde,
molti anni dopo avrei scoperto che
così scriveva abitualmente
il poeta da me più amato in giovinezza,
stelle marine gnomi agresti fate celesti
e turchine, ebbrezza d'azzurri fiori
erano le parole che coloravano
il mio foglio tutto, d'ogni
vocabolo appena vergato m'innamoravo
e trovavo offensivo, emotivo com'ero,
ogni gratuita violenza; mi pareva
fosse giusto eliminare ogni spreco
di parole che non fossero
necessarie al mio gioco:
quello solo contava finché durava
Gioco unico e assoluto
che alimentava quel mio poco-tutto dare
e avere, tutto il mio timido vivere.

Monte Porzio, febbraio 1989

A Little Song

There was a time when I used to write
with a fountain pen and green ink;
years later I discovered that
the poet I most admired in my youth
had the same habit of writing;
images of starfish, pastoral elves, azure
and aquamarine fairies, intoxicating blue flowers
dappled my entire page; I fell in love with
every word etched on paper
and took offense – emotional as I was –
at gratuitous violence; I felt justified
in disposing of every wasted
word that was not integral
to my game:
while it lasted, nothing else mattered:
The game – absolute and singular –
that nourished my small-all giving
and taking, all my timidity in living.

Monte Porzio, February 1989

Terra del Tempo

C'invase la stessa luce compatta
a tagli sui numerosi tornanti
fino allo scrigno finale: il nostro
paese del tempo arroccato lassù
in una sua forte e flebile demenza
"le stradine hanno ancora l'acciottolato antico"
e l'insegna sbilenca del Presepe
ancora un invito
sempre più irraggiungibile, irreale
irrelato. Poi un ennesimo vicolo
mai attraversato ma forse
da te già prefigurato. Anch'esso
ci avrebbe portato all'antico Castello
ne conoscevamo ormai ogni anfratto
o avello, ogni minaccia
di precipizio nello sprofondo.

Ma d'improvviso
sbucammo su una piazzola sguincia
a strapiombo sul mare
una ragazza seduta su una seggiola
accecata dal sole e dal vento
giocava silenziosamente a carte
di fronte a quell'azzurro immane, io
facevo fatica ad accettare una tale
disposizione naturale, tanto flagrante
da sembrarmi messinscena predisposta
angolo d'infanzia reinventata
e dunque non osai rivolgerle parola
temendo che quella visione

Land of Time

Pervaded by the same dense shafts of light
over the countless twists and turns
on our way to the ultimate treasure: our
town of time fortified there on the hill
in a powerful and feeble madness
"the little streets still have their ancient cobblestones"
and the crooked Nativity sign
still reads as an invitation
though ever more unreal, unreachable,
unconnected. Then a passage you may have previously
envisioned before but never before traversed.

That path would have led to the Castle too
by now we knew every burrow
and lair, every threat of
plummeting into the chasm.

But suddenly
we came upon a small sloped piazza
with a sheer drop to the sea
a young girl blinded by sun and wind
was sitting on a chair
silently playing cards
before that enormous sweep of azure, while
I had difficulty in believing
such a natural pose, so deliberate
that it seemed to me a staged scene
a corner of childhood imagined anew
and so I didn't dare speak to her
fearing that the vision

potesse di colpo svanire
forse le avrei chiesto soltanto
di condurci per mano
in quel suo regno d'acqua e di vento
in cambio degli occhi
che non ci sarebbero più serviti.

Infine il Castello scempiato
rimasto a metà dal vecchio frantumato
e dal nuovo incapace a rinascere
o riproporsi ad altro destino
un po' pateticamente
come quei disegni sui muri
chissà da quali mani dipinti
che vanno sfumando col tempo.
Siamo come questi murales, pensai,
che vanno sbiadendo un poco ogni anno.

Più tardi volli tornare sulla piazzola
ma la ragazza cieca mariposa era scomparsa
e con lei svanito tutto l'infantile armamentario.
Chiesi a un tale, che m'era stato indicato
come proprietario, se una casa sbrindellata
lì nei pressi fosse in vendita:
m'era messo in testa di comprarla
quella scassata bicocca.
Ci saremmo venuti periodicamente
a ricomporre qualche brandello
dei tanti noi stessi disseminati
in quella Terra del Tempo, lassù
dove il calendario

might suddenly vanish
perhaps I only wanted to ask her
to take us by the hand and lead us
into her kingdom of waters and wind
in exchange for our eyes
that would serve us no more.

Finally, the ruined Castle
suspended between the crumbling old
and the new, unable to resurrect itself
or claim a new destiny
how pathetic
like the images on its walls
painted by an unknown hand
fading with time
We resemble those murals, I thought,
a little fainter year by year.

Later I wanted to return to the small piazza
but the blind girl the mariposa was gone
and with her had vanished all her whimsical accoutrements.
I asked a fellow, whom I was told was the owner,
if that shabby house nearby
was for sale:
I had gotten into my head the notion
of buying that rundown shack.
We would return there from time to time
to reassemble a few shards
of our many selves scattered
in that Land of Time, up there
where the calendar

riporta sempre l'identico giorno
e ogni giorno è una pagina bianca
da riempire con le stesse parole.

Il nostro quaderno
è rimasto aperto su un tavolo
di fronte a una finestra a picco sul mare
su di esso batte impavido il sole
imbiancando ogni volta quella pagina
su cui ostinatamente noi ritorniamo
a scrivere lo stesso dettato:
O azzurra memoria che si consuma in se stessa!

Di ritorni dunque è fatta la vita
o agra ballatetta,
di false ripetizioni, vecchie e nuove,
come nei piccoli passi, incerti e pur certi
della nostra bambina-staffetta
che di colpo vince ogni malattia del tempo
e va sicura incontro al vento
rifiutando la mano
di chi l'ha portata fino lassù.

Fiumefreddo Bruzio, luglio-agosto 1989

always displays the same day
and every day is a blank page
to be filled with the same words.
Our notebook
remained open on the table
by a window overlooking the sea
where the intrepid sun beats down on it
blanching over and over again that page
to which we stubbornly return
to rewrite the same inscription:
O self-consuming azure memory!

Thus, life is composed of returns
O bitter little ballad
of false repetitions, new and old,
like the small steps, unsteady yet sure,
of our child-messenger
who suddenly overcomes every malady of time
and strides confidently against the wind
rejecting the hand
of the one who led her there.

Fiumefreddo Bruzio, July-August 1989

Grand Central

Grandioso, cupo ventre-cattedrale
di un finto Vicino Oriente
moschea di maschere vaganti
corse di ratti matti
oggi ritrovati improvvisamente
io quasi fresco *e calmo di falsa morte*
in questa barocca barca
che sbraca acqua scura fetida
mi rotolano addosso risate chiacchiere improperi
mentre m'inabisso e spappolo
sempre più... franano
le false colonne franano le false
balconate i lastroni alle finestre
i manifesti i cornicioni i lampadari
esplodono i barboni bambocci
accartocciati sui cartoni
volano le insegne i finti stili e steli
cadono lentamente ad una ad una
le belle stelle in schiera
da una lontana azzurra bandiera.

New York, 16 novembre 1989, h.23,15

Grand Central

Immense, dark cathedral-womb
of an imitation Near-Eastern
mosque of wanderer's icons
tracks of mad rats
retraced unwittingly today
I, almost like new, and *calm from my false death*
in this Baroque barge
that releases dirty fetid water
insults laughter chatter roll over me
while I'm engulfed and crushed
forever... the fake columns
collapse the fake balconies
the window panes the placards
the cornices the chandeliers all collapse
the homeless – rag dolls curled up in
their cardboard boxes – explode
signs imitative styles and stele fly by
slowly from a distant blue flag
one by one
the lovely stars in formation fall.

New York, November 16, 1989, 11:15 p.m.

Su una di queste panchine
venni a sedermi anch'io giovinetto
insieme a un'aggraziata gazzella

bella di labbra carnose
rosso rossetto odoroso
occhi di nera luce.

Sulle sue vaghe risposte alle mie
impacciate profferte
il giorno dopo avrei chiesto lumi

ad Amilcare autista della ditta
presso cui lavoravo anch'io part-time:
era da tutti ritenuto

provetto e sperto amatore. Non sapevo
che di lì a poco non l'avrei più rivista
sapevo ancora così poco io di sesso e d'amore.

Roma (giardinetti presso S.Paolo fuori le Mura), 17 maggio 1990

On one of these benches
I too once sat as a young man
with a graceful gazelle

lovely, with full lips
lipstick rosy-red scented
her eyes a black light.

To divine her hesitant responses
to my timid advances
tomorrow I would talk to

Amilcare the driver at the company
where I worked part-time:
known by all to be a proven expert

in love. I didn't know that
soon I would not see her again,
so little did I understand of love and desire.

Rome (Gardens of San Paolo fuori le Mura), May 17, 1990

Ti rivedo, Mendoza,
come un tulipano spavaldo
la sigaretta di sghimbescio
e il tuo mezzo sorriso acquatico.
Tempo n'è passato da quella mattina
affogata nel sole agostano.

Ti rivedo, Mendoza,
quasi gnomo che va rimpicciolendo
nella tua bara di carta
senza più storia
mentre invano un bambino va correndo
fra una stanza e l'altra della memoria.

Salerno, agosto 1990

I see you again, Mendoza,
bold as a tulip
your cigarette askew
and your watery half-smile.
Time has passed since that morning
drowned in August sun.

I see you again, Mendoza,
elfin, almost, shriveling
in your paper casket
bereft of history
a child running hopelessly
from room to room in our memory.

Salerno, August 1990

Rêverie

Rivedo il cerchio che spingevo a gara
per il sorriso d'una bambina
affacciata alla finestra.
Sembra quasi la stessa primavera
come quando andavo
svagato verso la mia scuola.
Ma oggi non è primavera
e non vado più a scuola.
I nostri aquiloni sfidano il vento
su sempre più su
mentre una voce amica risuona insistente
e di colpo si fa viso
d'un compagno di banco morto
senza rimpianto perché senza preavviso.
Quella mattina volevo morire anch'io
pensando alla carezza che come lui
anch'io avrei ricevuto da mia madre.

East Setauket, 8 dicembre 1990

Reverie

I see it again: the hoop I spun vying
for a little girl's smile
as she peered out the window.
It seems the same spring
as when I used to depart daydreaming
on my way to school.
But today is not spring
and I no longer go to school.
Our kites defy the wind
rising higher and higher
as a warm voice steadily resonates
and suddenly becomes the face
of an old school chum who passed away
without warning and thus without regret.
That morning I too wanted to die
imagining the caress I would receive
from my mother as he had.

East Setauket, December 8, 1990

Era un vecchio scannato scotennato
magro chiodo e solo
come una panchina deserta.
Seduto su una bilancia automatica
smangiava un esile panino
quasi invisibile la gente attorno
sciamanava inutilmente.
Appena all'altezza della sua testa
si leggeva questo cartello
Quel est ton poids aujourd'hui?

Parigi, Gare de Lyon, luglio 1991

He was an old-timer butchered and flayed
rail thin and forlorn
as a deserted bench.
Sitting on an electronic scale,
gnawing on a crust of bread
almost nonexistent to everyone around
he was wasting into oblivion.
Just above his head
a sign read
Quel est ton poids aujourd'hui?

Paris, Gare de Lyon, July 1991

Un tempo ero esile e gentile
come un cardello sperso nella fronda
recitavo canzonette e
giocavo a fare il bravo bambino.
A tutto credevo e di tutto
ero principe e servo
un coacervo di paure notturne
e arditezze diurne:
"Ti sfido, vento", detto talora d'inverno
mentre correvo su per la salita
di Sàbato de Vita.
Amavo mia madre d'un amore
eccessivo, per lei ero pronto a morire
per un niente e in ogni istante del giorno.
Innamorato di Elvira
che abitava al piano di sotto
non glielo dissi mai
non sapevo come si facesse
una dichiarazione d'amore, le sorridevo,
una finestra ammiccava all'altra e
tanto bastava a nutrire il mio errore.

East Setauket, settembre 1991

There was a time when I was thin and fragile
like a goldfinch lost among the leaves
I recited little songs
and played at being good.
I believed in all and was
the prince and servant of all
a bundle of terrors at night
and challenges by the day:
"I dare you, wind," I'd sometimes say
during winter running up the hill
on Sàbato de Vita.
I loved my mother with a love
of excess; for her I was ready to die
over nothing and at any moment of the day.
I was enamored with Elvira
who lived on the floor below.
I never told her,
I didn't know how
to declare my heart; I'd smile at her –
one window gesturing to the other –
and that was enough to feed my illusion.

East Setauket, September 1991

Termini-Alalà

Alla stazione
in un'arietta pungente che
tradiva gli scompensi di stagione.
Malanime affannate o tali credute
scimunivano ovunque
mentre da un altro binario
mille piedi vermi in continuo movimento
appena intravisti da sotto un treno
sciorinavano l'insopportabile rosario
l'insano coro e rovo.

Roma, settembre 1992

Termini-Alalà

At the train station
where an edgy breeze
betrayed the change of seasons.
Sad souls, disturbed or believed to be,
doddered around everywhere
while from another track
thousands of feet in continuous motion, worms
barely glimpsed beneath the train
mad choir and tangle
displaying a hideous rosary.

Rome, September 1992

Una volta in più

Non si sbagliò quella gentile
annunciatrice – voce soft e suadente –
che nell'areo decollante salutandoci
confuse destinazione per destino
"Benvenuti ai passeggeri con *destino* a New York".
Qualcuno ridacchiò a quello sbaglio,
altri sùbito s'avvide
di come errore e imitazione
una volta in più regolavano tra loro
redini e incroci, sigilli ed effrazioni.

Roma-New York, novembre 1992

Once Again

She wasn't wrong – that polished
attendant (with a soft and pleasing voice)
who, in greeting us as the plane took off,
confused "destination" with "destiny":
"Welcome to all passengers whose *destiny* is New York."
Someone giggled at the gaffe,
others realized instantly
how error and juxtaposition alone
once again controlled
checkpoints and crossroads, agreements and infractions.

Rome-New York, November 1992

Amore impresente
insegnami a parlare senza parole
a gioire senza gioie
a trovare cori e colori sulle bianche superfici
di questa casa non mia
dimmi come rinvigorire i prati senz'erba
come aspirare i fiori senza profumo.
Amore impresente
amore che m'addormenti a occhi aperti
non darmi domani l'oggi che mi neghi.

Coram, novembre 1992

Absent love
teach me how to speak without words
to rejoice without joys
to discover a chorus of color in the white surface
of this house that is not mine
tell me how to regrow meadows without grass
how to smell flowers without scent
absent love
love that rocks me to sleep with my eyes open
don't give me tomorrow the today you withhold.

Coram, November 1992

Putnam 531

La casa che sorgeva in fondo alla strada
portò ad un tratto miele e fantasia
un alberetto da me piantato nel giardino
i tanti minuscoli torno torno rododendri
che sembravano parlare da un altro mondo
e quei sassi che andammo a caricarci
nei sobborghi di chissà dove...
Ogni tanto - sempre più di rado –
vado a trovarla
scorgendo la sciacallezza del tempo
il suo bricolage e lo stravolgersi
delle cose nelle cose.
Vado a trovarla, come ubbidendo a un rituale
a un ordine imperioso
che comanda alle gambe, più che alla mente,
d'incamminarsi per quella tortuosa
stradina, miccia lenta
che si dipana infocata fino
al luogo della non-esplosione, lì
al ceneratoio buio scannato
tromba di scale invitante
molo e moloch addormentato
carta velina su cui ricalcare
le figure della farandola
ridda d'ipotesi, fantascena,
pura azzurra memoria.

Cambridge-New York, dicembre 1992

Putnam 531

The house rising up at the street's end
suddenly offered honey and whimsy
the little tree I planted in the garden
all around the many tiny rhododendrons
seeming to speak from another world
and those stones we took back with us
to the suburbs of who knows where...
Sometimes – more and more seldom –
I return for a visit
aware of time's jackals
its tinkering and tampering
with things in and among themselves.
I return for a visit, as if obeying a ritual,
an imperious command
that orders my legs, rather than my mind,
to walk down that winding
little lane, a slow fuse
that unravels red-hot to the point of non-explosion,
where in the profound darkness of the ash pit
a stairwell beckons
a mole and sleeping Moloch
tissue paper on which to trace
the figures of a farandole
a tumult of theories, phantasmagoria,
pure azure memory.

Cambridge-New York, December 1992

La veglia dell'ultimo soldato

Fu misurato alla luce il suo tempo;
ma il regno della notte è senza tempo
e senza spazio.

-Novalis

Cade la pioggia
lapidi lasciate vuote
grigio soffice degli aliti
a guardare in alto i ricordi inverecondi
che strisciano lungo le pareti

letti sfatti pieghe giallastre
tende convesse lasciate a se stesse
riflesse sullo specchio dell'armadio
stasera qualcuno dovrà pur avvicinarsi al piano
che di sopra suona indisturbato

finestra di stelle aperta
all'orizzonte nero dello sguardo
quale spazio quale canto rarefatto
vaga nell'immensità del cuor mio

cade cade la pioggia baci gocce
valanghe di fiori sul tuo viso
o amata amante
se mai ti vedrò apparire
si fermerà la giostra il minuto
l'istante

i tuoi capelli sono fili d'erba
intrecciati su cui serpeggiano
i notturni raggi lunari e l'argento
del fiume che scivola lento violento
e buca le mie mani

Nightwatch of the Last Soldier

His time was marked by light;
but night's kingdom has neither time
nor space.

-Novalis

Rain falls
gravestones left barren
the soft gray of breath
gazing at shameless memories
that crawl along the walls

unmade beds yellowed creases
billowing curtains abandoned
reflected in the cabinet mirror
surely tonight someone must encounter the piano
whose undisturbed music plays upstairs

window of stars opened
onto the black horizon of vision
what space what rarefied song
roams in the immensity of my heart

rain falls falls kisses and droplets
avalanche of flowers veiling your face
O lover loved
if ever I will see you appear
the carousel will cease that instant
that moment

your tresses are braided blades of grass
over which
nightly moon rays coil and
the silver of the river glides – idle and violent
it pierces my hands

stamattina la piccola contrada s'apre
a canti e fiori selvatici
come il solitario passeggiatore di Fraüenfeld
me ne andrò a spasso fermandomi
a ogni portone a ogni botteguccia
a ogni squarcio
di mondo-cortile mentre
il sole è una margherita gentile

è festa è festa nella piazza bianca tersa
festoni parole da un canto all'altro
si rinnova il bagno di luce e rumori
il bagno di luce e di rumori si rinnova

obliquo scende il raggio
meridiano nella stanza assonnata
nell'altra chi ha dimenticato quel divano rosso cupo?
e le sedie? e quel piano aperto?
Tristano è partito
tubano i due pappagallini ignari
la luce resta diagonale e tutto posa

due farfalle inseguono
i fiocchi di neve nel cortile
impazzite di freddo e di gioia
l'una all'altra vicine
sbatte dimentica una finestra
mentre il sangue scorre allegro
dalle mie ginocchia bambine

partiranno tra non molto i miei ospiti blasonati
antenati vestiti di tutto punto
hanno rallegrato le mie ultime ore
spariranno così come d'un tratto
arrivarono ed io dissipatore distinto
rientrerò nel mio dipinto

this morning the tiny hamlet opens up
to chants and wildflowers
like the lone wayfarer of Fraüenfeld
I will stroll and stop
at every door at every shop
at every fracture
of the courtyard-world while
the sun is a gentle daisy

there's a dance a dance in the pristine white square
garlands chatter everywhere
the pool of lights and sounds renews itself
it renews itself

obliquely the midday rays fall
into the sleep-lulled room
elsewhere, who has forgotten the crimson sofa?
the easy chairs? the open piano?
Tristan is gone
the two little parrots are cooing unawares
the light slants and everything stands still

two butterflies chase
the snowflakes in the courtyard
wild with cold and joy
huddled together
a forgotten window slams shut
while blood flows cheerfully
from my youthful knees

soon my aristocratic guests will leave
my ancestors in full regalia
who have enlivened my last hours
will disappear as suddenly as they arrived
and I, the refined and dissipated one,
will re-enter the realm of my painting

in cantina l'atro concerto
s'adagia nel brillìo metallico
degli strumenti campestri
ammassati in un angolo
a sé lasciati gli uni agli altri

a passi felpati giungerà tra breve l'alba
il cielo purissimo cupo riazzurra
cancellerà ogni demenza
una vetrata di colpo s'alluma
e chiede venia l'acqua
della sua esistenza.
L'acqua che precipita
ruzzola capitombola sballotta
sbanda rotola danza ritorna
sui sassi sbatacchia sballa
mulinella pisteggia sbuca
riciarla sdrucciola e
lieve
lieve
svana

muore infine la notte
imbuto profondo stellato
un grande magnifico tondo
copre una volta in più
i miei segni di sabbia
e il Niente che mi fa Tutto
a questo mondo.

St. Jean-de-Valériscle - Sound Beach, luglio 1999

in the cellar the morose concert
settles into the metallic glint
of quaint instruments
amassed in a corner
left all to themselves

with hushed steps soon will come the dawn
the purest sky from dim to blue shimmers again
erasing every bit of madness
a windowpane suddenly lights up
and water asks forgiveness
for its existence
the water that rushes
tumbles rolls jolts
slides spins dances returns
over rocks bangs dashes
whirls races springs
chatters slips and
softly
softly
vanishes

finally the night dies
in this profound starry sky
a great majestic ring
covers once more
my marks in the sand
and the Nothingness that makes me Whole
in this world.

St. Jean-de-Valériscle - Sound Beach, July 1999

Scrivere è rivelare agli altri qualcosa
che agli altro noto non sia
ignoto perciò anche a noi stessi
che l'abbiamo or ora scoperto, invenìto.
Sarà forse una cosa modesta
eppure quella modesta cosa brilla risuona
c'invade un momento la vita
o ci abbandona.

Macerata, giugno 1992

To write is to reveal to others
something not known to them
unknown even to ourselves
something just discovered or now envisioned.
A simple thing, perhaps,
and yet a simple thing that glows, resounds,
that for a moment invades our lives
or abandons us.

Macerata, June 1992

NOTES

Ceres

To the Reader
The evocation of "my fraternal, hypocritical reader" is an allusion to Charles Baudelaire's "hypocrite lecteur" in *Les fleurs du mal.*

Looking out from this oval summit
"All-nature" is a translation of the Italian *tuttanatura*, a neologism created by Fontanella. The poet often joins two existing words to form a new linguistic expression.

Sequence for My Father
The "Lambretta" was one of the most popular Italian mopeds in the '50s.

For Love
"Just as the poet told" is an allusion to *La pioggia nel pineto,* a famous poem by Gabriele D'Annunzio (1863-1938).

For Francesco Paolo Memmo (I)
Francesco Paolo Memmo is a poet and longtime friend of the author.

A Weakness Tonight
According to Fontanella, the mannequin is the author himself, who feels removed from the reality of the outside world.

To find you again by chance, if only for a moment
Fontanella has explained that the "Gray Egg" is a metaphor for the sense of suffocation and constraint that he endured while living in a small apartment, so small that he felt as if he were inside a tiny egg.
The phrase "I search for the Interior" is taken from the title of a painting by Gianfranco Baruchello, who, in turn, took the expression from a letter by Antonin Artaud to a friend.

Neapolitan Moonlight
The title appears in English in the original Italian version. The poem is dedicated to Maurizio Vignola, a long-time friend of the author.

For Romolo Runcini
This poem was inspired by a walk that the poet took late at night in Naples with his friend Romolo Runcini, a university professor.

Quivering whisper of a tree in full blossom
"White-walled" is a translation of the Italian neologism *biancasala*.

Stanzas for Emma

The poems in this section are dedicated to Emma, the poet's daughter, born on October 4, 1987. They were written during the first four years of Emma's life, when she remained in Italy with her mother while Fontanella was living in New York but visited his family often.

XV
"All-present" is a translation of the Italian neologism *Tuttopresente*.

XIX
"Gilded-Yellow" and "Sighing-Green" translate respectively the Italian neologisms *Gialloro* and *Verdesospiroso*.

XXI
The Italian term *anarrosi* derives from the Greek and indicates a reflux, a force of inertia.

XXIII
Vasco Graca Moura (1948) is a contemporary Portuguese writer and poet, who has translated *The Divine Comedy*, among other works, into Portuguese. Fontanella was inspired to write this poem to Emma after reading verses by Moura.

XXVI
Gavroche is the young and brave hero in Victor Hugo's *Les Miserables*.

Ars Poetica

The title of this section, *Ars Poetica*, refers to the famous work by the Latin poet Horace.

There's the visible
The Italian *mostro* is derived from the Latin *monstrum*, which means divine sign or prodigy. We have used the word "Demon" rather than "Monster" in our translation to suggest a spiritual dimension and to avoid any possible association with horror movies that the word "Monster" might have for American readers.

For Pier Paolo Pasolini
Pier Paolo Pasolini (1922-1975), writer, poet, and film director, was one of the leading figures in the Italian cultural and political landscape after World War II.

When suddenly in this Virginian light
The subject of this poem is poetry, which is a feminine noun in Italian. Here, as in the following poem, "Resisting Time Present," we decided to use the feminine pronoun "she" to refer to "poetry."

For Achille Serrao
The author wrote this poem after a visit, with his friend Achille Serrao, to Pico Farnese, hometown of Tommaso Landolfi (1907-1986), a writer particularly dear to Fontanella. The Solitary Dweller is Tommaso Landolfi. The last two lines are taken from a poem by Silvio D'Arzo.

Resisting Time Present
Fontanella met Michel Deguy, a well-known contemporary French poet, when the latter gave two lectures at State University of New York, Stony Brook, where Fontanella teaches. Deguy's presence inspired the author to write this poem, the topic of which is poetry itself.
The phrase *"many comings all together"* appears in English in the original.

Ballads and Songs

Song for Paolo Conte
Paolo Conte is one of the most renowned Italian singers and songwriters (*cantautore*) from the same Genoese tradition as Umberto Bindi, Luigi Tenco, Gino Paoli, Sergio Endrigo, Ivano Fossati, and Bruno Lauzi.

Chimera
The poem is dedicated to Mario Luzi, Fontanella's good friend who is considered by many critics to be the most significant contemporary Italian poet. The

poem is strongly influenced by the work of two other Italian writers – Dino Campana and Antonio Delfini. *Chimera* was originally published in *Per Mario Luzi* (Edited by Teresa Lazzaro, Catanzaro, Ed. Rubbettino, 1989), a small anthology of poems dedicated to Luzi, written by various contemporary Italian poets such as Alessandro Parronchi, Maria Luisa Spaziani, and Piero Bigongiari.

A Little Song
"The poet I most admired in my youth" is an allusion to Giuseppe Ungaretti (1888-1970).

Grand Central
The title refers to Grand Central train station in New York, where the poem was written. The line *calmo di falsa morte* ("calm from my false death") is a quote from the writer Tommaso Landolfi.

He was an old timer butchered and flayed
"*Quel est ton poids aujourd'hui?*": "How much do you weigh today?"

There was a time when I was thin and fragile
Sabato De Vita is the name of the narrow street in Fratte (in the province of Salerno) where the poet lived from 1951 to 1956.

Termini-Alalà
Termini is the name of the major train station in Rome. At the time that the station was built, *Alalà* was a commonly used exclamation in the Fascist regime, and here serves as an ironic reference to that period.

Once Again
The adjective *soft* appears in English in the Italian version.

Absent Love
We have used "absent" as a translation for the Italian neologism *impresente*, since comparable terms in English, such as "non-present" or "impresent," are awkward. However, the poet's intent is to convey the idea of a love that is not present, which has a slightly different emphasis than the term "absent" implies.

Putnam 531
The title refers to the poet's address in Cambridge, Massachusetts, where he lived from 1980 to 1982.
The *farandola* (frenzied dance) is a chain dance from Provence.

ABOUT THE AUTHOR

Luigi Fontanella (Salerno, Italy, 1943) studied at the University of Rome and at Harvard University (Ph.D. in Romance Languages and Literatures). He has served as a Fulbright Fellow (Princeton University, 1976-1978), and has taught at Columbia, Princeton, and Wellesley College. Presently he is Professor of Italian at the State University of New York, Stony Brook. Fontanella has published ten books of poetry, two books of fiction, and six books of criticism.

POETRY: *La verifica incerta* (Roma: De Luca, 1972); *La vita trasparente* (Venezia: Rebellato, 1978); *Simulazione di reato* (Manduria: Lacaita, 1979); *Fabula* (1979, with drawings by Gianfranco Baruchello, Roma: Ediz. Carte Segrete, 1979); *Convenevoli d'uso* (1980, with Mario Lunetta, Bergamo: Il Bagatto, 1980); *Stella Saturnina* (Roma: Il Ventaglio, 1989); *Round Trip* (Udine: Campanotto, 1991, Ragusa Prize 1993); *Parole per Emma* (Salerno: Edisud, 1991); *From G. to G.: 101 Somnets* (New York: Peter Lang, 1996, with Giose Rimanelli); *Ceres* (Formia: Caramanica Ed., 1996, Orazio Caputo Prize, Olindo de Gennaro Prize, and Pianiga-San Martino Prize); *Terra del Tempo* (Bologna: Book Editore, 2000, Circe Sabaudia Prize, Minturnae Prize, S.Andrea Prize, and S. Nicola Arcella Prize).

NARRATIVE: *Milestone e altre storie* (Siena: Messapo, 1983); *Hot Dog* (novel, Roma: Bulzoni, 1986, now available in English translation by Justin Vitiello, Lewiston, New York: Soleil Ed., 1998).

CRITICISM: *I campi magnetici di A.Breton-P.Soupault* (Roma: Newton Compton, 1979); *Il surrealismo italiano* (Roma: Bulzoni, 1983); *Tozzi in America* (Roma: Bulzoni, 1986); *La parola aleatoria* (Firenze: Le Lettere, 1992); *The Literary Journal as a Cultural Witness* (Stony Brook, New York: Filibrary Press, 1996, co-edited with Luca Somigli); *Storia di Bontempelli* (Ravenna: Longo Editore, 1997).

Founder and President of the Italian Poetry Society of America (IPSA), Fontanella is the editor of *Gradiva*, an international journal of Italian literature.

ABOUT THE TRANSLATORS

Carol Lettieri and **Irene Marchegiani Jones** have previously worked together on the translation of *Star of Free Will*, a collection of poetry by Maria Luisa Spaziani published by Guernica in 1996.

Carol Lettieri is a San Francisco-based writer and editor, who writes on travel, architecture, education, and technology. Her travel articles on Italy have appeared in *The New York Times* and *The Los Angeles Times,* among other publications. In addition to *Star of Free Will*, she has also translated *Omneros* by Mohammed Dib, a bilingual English/French edition of poetry published by Red Hill Press. Ms. Lettieri has an M.A. in Comparative Literature from the University of California, Irvine, and has studied Italian literature in Italy, while living in Florence.

Irene Marchegiani Jones is Professor of Italian at the California State University, Long Beach. She is the co-author of the Italian reader *Incontri Attuali* and the texbook *Crescendo!* In addition to working on issues related to second-language acquisition and the teaching of the Italian language, she has written articles on women writers, Giacomo Leopardi, and modern and contemporary Italian literature. She has published some of her poetry in Italian journals and has translated Torquato Tasso's *Aminta* (New York: Italica Press, 2000) with Prof. Charles Jernigan.
She is co-editor (with Tom Haeussler) of *The Poetics of Place. Florence Imagined* (Florence: Leo. S. Olschki Editore, 2000), a collection of essays addressing issues related to the fictional and imaginary dimensions of literary representations of Florence.